THE FEDERAL GRAND JURY

THE FEDERAL GRAND JURY

CHARLES DOYLE

Nova Science Publishers, Inc.
New York

For permission to use material from this book please contact us:
Telephone 631-231-7269; Fax 631-231-8175
Web Site: http://www.novapublishers.com

LIBRARY OF CONGRESS CATALOGING-IN-PUBLICATION DATA

Doyle, Charles.
The federal grand jury / Charles Doyle.
p. cm.
Includes bibliographical references and index.
ISBN 978-1-60456-985-8 (softcover)
1. Grand jury--United States. I. Title.
KF9642.D69 2009
345.73'072--dc22

2008036570

Published by Nova Science Publishers, Inc. ✢ New York

CONTENTS

PREFACE

The federal grand jury exists to investigate crimes against the United States and to secure the constitutional right of grand jury indictment. Its responsibilities require broad powers.

As an arm of the United States District Court which summons it, upon whose process it relies, and which will receive any indictments it returns, the grand jury's subject matter and geographical jurisdiction is that of the court to which it is attached.

Ordinarily, the law is entitled to everyone's evidence. Witnesses subpoenaed to appear before the grand jury, therefore, will find little to excuse their appearance. Once before the panel, however, they are entitled to benefit of various constitutional, common law and statutory privileges including the right to withhold self-incriminating testimony and the security of confidentiality of their attorney-client communications. They are not, however, entitled to have an attorney with them in the grand jury room when they testify.

The grand jury conducts its business in secret. Those who attend its sessions may ordinarily disclose its secrets only when the interests of justice permit.

Unless the independence of the grand jury is overborne, irregularities in the grand jury process ordinarily will not result in dismissal of an indictment, particularly where dismissal is sought after conviction.

The concurrence of the attorney for the government is required for the trial of any indictment voted by the grand jury. In the absence of such an endorsement or when a panel seeks to report, the court enjoys narrowly exercised discretion to dictate expungement or permit distribution of the report.

In: The Federal Grand Jury
Editor: C. Doyle
ISBN: 978-1-60456-985-8

Chapter 1

THE FEDERAL GRAND JURY*

INTRODUCTION

"The grand jury [has] a unique role in our criminal justice system."[1] It was born of a desire to identify more criminals for prosecution and thereby to increase the King's revenues. But the exclusive power to accuse is also the power not to accuse and early on the grand jury became both the "sword and the shield of justice."[2]

This dual character marks the federal grand jury to this day. As the sword of justice, it enjoys virtually unfettered power to secretly investigate the mere possibility that federal laws may have been broken. Yet it remains a potential shield for it must give its approval before anyone may be brought to trial for a serious federal crime.[3]

What follows is a brief general description of the federal grand jury, with particular emphasis on its more controversial aspects – relationship of the prosecutor and the grand jury, the rights of grand jury witnesses, grand jury secrecy, and rights of targets of a grand jury investigation.

BACKGROUND

The grand jury is an institution of antiquity. When William the Conqueror sought to compile the Domesday Book, he called upon the most respected men of each community. Their reports were collected to form an inventory of England's property, real and personal, and served as the

* Excerpted from CRS Report 95-1135, dated January 22, 2008.

foundation of the Crown's tax rolls. Almost a century later in the Assize of Clarendon, the ancestor of the modern grand jury, Henry II used the same approach to unearth reports of crime,[4] and thereby increase the flow of fines and forfeitures into his treasury.[5]

From the power to accuse, the power to refuse to accuse eventually developed. By the American colonial period, the grand jury had become both an accuser and a protector. It was the protector the Founders saw when they enshrined the grand jury within the Bill of Rights and the reason it has been afforded extraordinary inquisitorial powers and exceptional deference.[6]

The Fifth Amendment right to grand jury indictment is only constitutionally required in federal cases.[7] In a majority of the states prosecution may begin either with an indictment or with an information or complaint filed by the prosecutor.[8]

Although abolition of the right to indictment in the states and abolition of the grand jury itself in England were primarily matters of judicial efficiency,[9] most of the more contemporary proposals to change the federal grand jury system are the product of concern for the fairness of the process or for perceived excesses caused by prosecutorial exuberance.[10]

ORGANIZATIONAL MATTERS

Jurisdiction

The authority of a federal grand jury is sweeping, but it is limited to the investigation of possible violations of federal criminal law triable in the district in which it is sitting.[11] This does not include the power to investigate conduct known to have no connection to the court's jurisdiction, but does encompass the authority to inquire whether such a connection may exist.[12]

The grand jury may begin its examination even in the absence of probable cause or any other level of suspicion that a crime has been committed within its reach. In the exercise of its jurisdiction, the grand jury may "investigate merely on suspicion that the law is being violated, or even just because it wants assurance that it is not,"[13] and its inquiries "may be triggered by tips, rumors, evidence proffered by the prosecutor, or the personal knowledge of the grand jurors."[14]

Unrestrained "by questions of propriety or forecasts of the probable result of the investigation or by doubts whether any particular individual will be found properly subject to an accusation,"[15] its "investigation is not fully carried out until every available clue has been run down and all witnesses examined in every proper way to find if a crime has been committed."[16]

Selection

The various United States District Courts are instructed to order one or more grand juries to be summoned when the public interest requires.[17] In addition, the Attorney General may request the District Court to summon a special grand jury in any of the larger districts or when he or she believes the level of criminal activity in the district warrants it.[18]

Historically, the responsibility of choosing those to be named to the grand jury fell to the sheriff.[19] Selection of the members of the grand jury by the sheriff of the county continued for some time and was used generally in colonial America, although grand jurors were elected in some colonies.[20]

At one time, the law governing the selection, qualifications and exemptions of federal grand jurors was determined largely by reference to the law of the state in which the grand jury was to be convened.[21] These matters are now the responsibility of the court, governed by the Jury Selection and Service Act of 1968,[22] and the selection plan established for the district in which the grand jury is to be convened.

Federal grand jurors must be citizens of the United States, eighteen years of age or older and residents of the judicial district for at least a year, be able to read, write and understand English with sufficient proficiency to complete the juror qualification form, be able to speak English, and be mentally and physically able to serve; those facing pending felony charges and those convicted of a felony (if their civil rights have not been restored) are ineligible.[23]

Discrimination in selection on the basis of race, color, religion, sex, national origin, or economic status is prohibited,[24] and grand jurors must be "selected at random from a fair cross section of the community in the district or division wherein the court convenes."[25] Either a defendant, an attorney for the government, or a member of an improperly excluded group may challenge the selection of a grand jury panel contrary to these requirements.[26]

Since the grand jury began with indictments based upon the personal knowledge of the members of the panel, there is some historical justification for the position that bias or want of impartiality should not disqualify a potential grand juror. The drafters of the Federal Rules of Criminal

Procedure seemed to confirm this view when they rejected proposed language permitting a challenge of the grand jury based on "bias or prejudice."[27]

One commentator points out, however, that language in several Supreme Court cases has led some lower courts to assert that grand juries must be unbiased, or at least they must not be exposed to improper influences that would create bias.[28] The case law also seems to focus on any contamination of the panel as a whole and to rely upon each grand juror's faithfulness to his or her oath to avoid the adverse consequences of individual bias.[29]

Grand jury panels consist of sixteen to twenty-three members,[30] sixteen of whom must be present for a quorum,[31] and twelve of whom must concur to indict.[32] The size of grand jury panels is a remnant of the common law,[33] but the common law treatises and the cases provide little indication of why those particular numbers were chosen.[34] Of course, when the grand jury's accusations were based primarily upon the prior knowledge of the panel's members, larger panels were more understandable.

The movement which lead to abolition of the right to indictment in many of the states also resulted in a reduction in the size of most state grand jury panels.[35] Perhaps because of a reluctance to dilute the federal constitutional right to indictment, there have been few suggestions for a comparable reduction in the size of the federal grand jury.[36]

The selection of twenty-three members for a panel which requires only the presence of sixteen to conduct its business would seem to obviate the need for alternate grand jurors. This is not the case, however, and the rules permit the court to direct the selection of alternate grand jurors at the same time and in the same manner as other members of the panel are selected.[37]

Tenure

After selection, members of the grand jury are sworn in,[38] the court names a "foreperson and deputy foreperson,"[39] and instructs the grand jury.[40] Federal grand juries sit until discharged by the court, but generally not for longer than 18 months with the possibility of one six month extension.[41] Special grand juries convened in large districts or in districts with severe crime problems also serve until discharged or up to 18 months but may be extended up to 36 months and in some cases beyond.[42]

PROCEEDINGS BEFORE THE GRAND JURY

Grand Jury and the Prosecutor

The grand jury does not conduct its business in open court nor does a federal judge preside over its proceedings.[43] The grand jury meets behind closed doors with only the jurors, attorney for the government, witnesses, someone to record testimony, and possibly an interpreter present.[44]

In many cases, the government will have already conducted an investigation and the attorney for the government will present evidence to the panel. In other cases, the investigation will be incomplete and the grand jury, either on its own initiative or at the suggestion of the attorney for the government, will investigate.

Originally, the grand jury brought criminal accusations based exclusively on the prior knowledge of its members. Today, the grand jury acts on the basis of evidence presented by witnesses called for that purpose and only rarely on the personal knowledge of individual jurors.[45]

The attorney for the government will ordinarily arrange for the appearance of witnesses before the grand jury, will suggest the order in which they should be called, and will take part in questioning them.[46] The prosecutor is the most common source of legal advice and will draft most of the indictments returned by the grand jury.[47]

Subpoenas

Grand jury witnesses usually appear before the grand jury under subpoena.[48] The rule calls for subpoenas to be available in blank for the "parties" to the proceedings before the court, but "no one is meaningfully a party in a grand jury proceeding."[49] Nevertheless, there seems little question that subpoenas may be issued and served at the request of the panel itself,[50] although the attorney for the government ordinarily "fills in the blanks" on a grand jury subpoena and arranges the case to be presented to the grand jury.[51] Unjustified failure to comply with a grand jury subpoena may result in a witness being held in civil contempt,[52] convicted for criminal contempt,[53] or both.[54] A witness who lies to a grand jury may be prosecuted for perjury,[55] or for making false declarations before the grand jury.[56]

Conversely, others with information they wish to convey to the grand jury are prohibited from doing so except through the court or the attorney for the government.[57] Consequently neither a potential defendant nor a grand jury target nor any of their counsel has any right to appear before the grand jury unless invited or subpoenaed.[58] Nor does a potential defendant nor a grand jury target nor their counsel have any right to present exculpatory evidence to the grand jury nor substantive objection if the government fails to do so.[59]

Grand jury appearances, however, are more likely to be fought than sought. Resistance is ordinarily futile. Absent self-incrimination or some other privilege, the law expects citizens to cooperate with efforts to investigate crime.[60] In the name of this expectation a witness may be arrested, held for bail, and under some circumstances incarcerated.[61] Even when armed with an applicable privilege a witness' compliance with a grand jury subpoena is only likely to be excused with respect to matters protected by the privilege. A witness subpoenaed to testify rather than merely produce documents may be compelled to appear before the grand jury and claim the privilege with respect to any questions to which it applies.[62]

Witnesses also enjoy the benefit of fewer checks on the grand jury's exercise of investigative power than might be the case if the inquisitor were a government official rather than a group of randomly selected members of the community.[63] Thus as a general rule, the grand jury is entitled to every individual's evidence even though testimony may prove burdensome, embarrassing, or socially or economically injurious for the witness.[64]

A grand jury subpoena may even "trump" a pre-exist protective court order under some circumstances.[65] This is not to say that the grand jury's authority is without limit, or that excessive prosecutorial zeal before the grand jury is unknown, or that there is never any just cause for a witness's refusal to answer a question or provide a document, but simply that the restraints on the grand jury's authority have been narrowly drawn and applied.

Common Law Privileges

Grand jury subpoenas are subject to the maxim that, "the grand jury. . .may not itself violate a valid privilege, whether established by the Constitution, statutes, or the common law."[66] In the context of grand jury subpoenas, as in most others, federal evidentiary privileges are governed by the Federal Rules of Evidence.[67]

The Rules do not articulate specific privileges. Instead, they declare that federal law concerning privileges is "governed by the principles of the common law as they may be interpreted by the courts of the United States in the light of reason and experience."[68]

Although the standard is clearly evolutionary, present federal law seems to reflect three levels of privilege recognition. Some privileges like doctor-patient, have been refused recognition at least for the time being, some like journalist-source have been recognized for limited purposes that may or may not provide the basis for a motion to quash a grand jury subpoena, and some like clergy-communicant have been recognized as evidentiary privileges for grand jury purposes.

Thus, the federal courts have said that for purposes of federal law no evidentiary privilege exists in cases of:

- physician-patient;[69]
- accountant-client;[70]
- researcher-source;[71]
- parent-child;[72]
- employer-stenographer;[73]
- banker-depositor;[74]
- draft counselor-client;[75]
- police observation post location;[76]
- probation officer-probationer;[77]
- insurance company-client;[78]
- academic peer review;[79]
- medical peer review;[80]
- unwaivable confidentiality of child abuse and juvenile records;[81]
- agricultural loan mediation;[82]
- union officials-union members;[83]
- Secret Service protective function;[84]
- litigation settlement negotiations;[85]
- private investigator-client;[86]

A second group consists of recognized but qualified privileges, whose effectiveness against a grand jury subpoena may be uncertain at best. Members of the group include privileges for:

- journalists (not generally recognized for grand jury purposes);[87]
- critical self-evaluation;[88]
- presidential communications;[89]
- state legislators;[90]

- federal statutory privileges;[91]
- state secret/national security;[92]
- bank examiners;[93]
- state recognized privileges;[94]
- intra-agency, government deliberative process;[95] and
- ombudsman.[96]

The handful of privileges that provide the grounds for quashing a grand jury subpoena include:

- attorney-client;[97]
- attorney work product;[98]
- clergyman-communicant;[99]
- informer identity;[100]
- spousal immunity;[101]
- spousal communications;[102] and
- psychotherapist-patient.[103]

Perhaps the two most commonly cited privileges in motions to quash grand jury subpoenas are the attorney-client privilege and the closely related attorney work product privilege. The attorney-client privilege covers "[c]onfidential disclosures by a client to an attorney made in order to obtain legal assistance."[104] The privilege does not foreclose grand jury inquiry into attorney-client communications which are themselves criminal or are in furtherance of some future criminal activity.[105] Nor, as a general rule, does the privilege cover the identity of the client nor details concerning payment of the attorney's fee,[106] and thus the privilege will usually not constitute grounds to quash a grand jury subpoena directed to secure that information.[107]

This last general rule may be subject to any of three exceptions. The privilege may extend to information concerning the identity of the client or the particulars of the fee arrangement when (1) "disclosure would implicate the client in the very criminal activity for which legal advice was sought; . . . [(2)] disclosure of the client's identity by his attorney would have supplied the last link in an existing chain of incriminating evidence likely to lead to the client's indictment; . . . [or (3)] the payment of the fee itself is unlawful . . . [or] the fee contract contain[s] any confidential communication."[108]

The attorney "work product privilege protects any material obtained or prepared by a lawyer in the course of his legal duties, provided that the work was done with an eye toward litigation."[109] Like the attorney-client privilege it is subject to a crime/fraud exception.[110] Unlike that privilege, however, "the work product privilege belongs to both the client and the attorney, either one of whom may claim it. An innocent attorney may claim the privilege even if a prima facie case of fraud or criminal activity has been made as to the client."[111]

Constitutional Privileges

The cases which give rise to attorney-client and attorney work product claims not infrequently include Sixth Amendment invocations as well.[112] At first blush, the Sixth Amendment right to the assistance of counsel might be thought to afford but scant ground upon which to base a motion to quash a grand jury subpoena since the right does not ordinarily attach until an individual has been accused of a crime, i.e., after indictment.[113] This is in fact a very real limitation, but one which admits to exception where either the client has already been indicted or where the vitality of the right requires pre-attachment recognition.[114]

As a general rule, a grand jury subpoena will only be quashed on the basis of Sixth Amendment considerations on those rare instances where it is shown to have been motivated solely by an intent to harass, where compliance would unnecessarily result in an actual conflict of interest between the attorney and his or her client, or where compliance would unnecessarily tend to undermine the attorney-client relationship.[115] The Sixth Amendment, however, does not assure a grand jury witness of the right to have an attorney present when the witness testifies before the grand jury.[116]

A successful refusal to appear or testify before the grand jury, based upon the First Amendment guarantees of the freedoms of the press, association, or expression,[117] is even more rare. Under extreme circumstances, it will provide the grounds to avoid a contempt citation or to quash a federal grand jury subpoena,[118] ordinarily it will not.[119]

The Fourth Amendment prohibits unreasonable governmental searches and seizures.[120] What might be unreasonable under other circumstances, may well be considered reasonable in a grand jury environment. For example, grand jury subpoenas are not considered per se unreasonable simply because they require neither probable cause nor the filter of an approving neutral magistrate. The opportunity to be heard on a motion to quash before complying makes the grand jury subpoena in many respects less intrusive than the warrant.[121]

Even "forthwith" subpoenas, where the opportunity to quash may be minimized,[122] have generally been thought to pass constitutional muster, either because the party to whom they were address complied, *i.e.*, consented,[123] or because the circumstances presented exigencies similar to those to which Fourth Amendment demands have traditionally yielded.[124]

The shadow of the Fourth Amendment is visible in Rule 17(c) of the Federal Rules of Criminal Procedure, which supplies the grounds most often successfully employed to quash a grand jury subpoena:

- A subpoena may also command the person to whom it is directed to produce the books, papers, documents or other objects designated therein. The court on motion made promptly may quash or modify the subpoena if compliance would be unreasonable or oppressive.

However, a "'grand jury proceeding is accorded a presumption of regularity, which generally may be dispelled only upon particularized proof of irregularities in the grand jury process.' Consequently, a grand jury subpoena issued through normal channels is presumed to be reasonable."[125]

A subpoena is "unreasonable or oppressive" if (1) it commands the production of things clearly irrelevant to the investigation being pursued; (2) it fails to specify the things to be produced with reasonable particularity; or (3) it is unreasonable in terms of the relative extent of the effort required to comply.[126]

It is not unreasonable under the Fourth Amendment nor contrary to the Fifth Amendment privilege against self-incrimination to subpoena a witness to appear before the grand jury in order to furnish a voice exemplar,[127] a handwriting exemplar,[128] to sign a consent form authorizing the disclosure of bank records,[129] or for juveniles to produce a DNA sample and a complete set of fingerprints.[130] Consequently, the courts will not quash an otherwise valid subpoena issued for any those purposes.

Although the Fifth Amendment privilege against self-incrimination[131] precludes requiring a witness to testify at his or her criminal trial,[132] it does not "confer an absolute right to decline to respond in a grand jury inquiry."[133] Once before the grand jury, a witness may decline to present self-incriminating testimony.[134] The right does not include the option to protect pre-existing, voluntarily prepared personal papers on the ground that they are self-incriminatory,[135] but a witness may refused to produce that documents where the act of production (rather than the mere content of the documents) would itself be incriminating.[136] The privilege, nevertheless, is a personal one, and as a result provides no basis to quash a grand jury subpoena duces tecum for the records of corporate or other legal entities rather than of individuals.[137]

The Fifth Amendment due process clause,[138] with and like the unreasonable or oppressive standard of Rule 17, supplement other grounds for a motion to quash grand jury subpoenas when confronted with potential abuse of the grand jury process or practices that are fundamentally unfair. Thus, a grand jury subpoena is subject to a motion to quash if issued for the sole or dominant purpose of preparing the government's case against a previously indicted target, but not if there is a possible valid purpose for the subpoena.[139] Nor may the grand jury subpoena be used as a discovery device for civil cases in which the government has an interest.[140]

Finally, the Constitution provides that "for any speech or debate in either House, they [the members of Congress] shall not be questioned in any other place."[141] The privilege precludes questioning before the grand jury of a Member's legislative acts.[142]

Statutory and Other Limitations of Grand Jury Subpoena Authority

Federal law prohibits the use of evidence tainted by illegal wiretapping.[143] The prohibition provides just cause for the refusal of a grand jury witness to respond to inquiries based on illegal wiretapping information.[144] Similarly, a grand jury subpoena directed towards earlier testimony secured under a promise of immunity from prosecution may be quashed if sought solely for the purpose of indicting the witness.[145] Conflicting authority indicates the difficulty of determining whether particular statutes that classify information as confidential thereby take the information beyond the reach of a federal grand jury subpoena, or otherwise confine its authority.[146]

The vitality of regulatory limitations upon the grand jury subpoena power are equally unclear. The courts have consistently held that the government's failure to comply with the guidelines in the United States Attorneys' Manual concerning grand jury subpoenas does not constitute valid ground upon which to quash or modify a grand jury subpoena,[147] but implications of ethical rules purporting to proscribe the manner in which government attorneys may act with respect grand jury subpoenas and other matters arising out of their duties are less clear.[148]

Secrecy

Federal grand juries conduct their business in a secrecy defined by rules which limit who may attend,[149] and the circumstances under which matters involving the conduct of their business may be disclosed.[150] Grand jury secrecy predates the arrival of the grand jury in this country and the Supreme Court has said that "the proper functioning of our grand jury system depends upon" it.[151] On the other hand, it has always been freely acknowledged that there are circumstances when, in balancing the interests of justice, the interests to be served by disclosure will outweigh the interests in secrecy.

The cloak surrounding the grand jury's business serves several interests:

> (1) to prevent the escape of those whose indictment may be contemplated; (2) to insure the utmost freedom to the grand jury in its deliberations, and to prevent persons subject to indictment or their friends from importuning the grand jurors; (3) to prevent subornation of perjury or tampering with the witness who may testify before [the] grand jury and later appear at the trial of those indicted by it; (4) to encourage free and untrammeled disclosures by persons who have information with respect to the commission of crimes; (5) to protect [the] innocent accused who is exonerated from disclosure of the fact that he has been under investigation and from the expense of standing trial where there was no probability of guilt.[152]

Conversely, circumstances may exist under which evidence of what occurred before the grand jury could prevent a miscarriage of justice or serve some other public interest. These conditions may develop in any environment in which evidence unearthed by the grand jury might be relevant. They can arise in the federal criminal trials which often follow from a grand jury investigation, in state criminal investigations and proceedings, in civil litigation, and in administrative and legislative proceedings.

The boundaries of grand jury secrecy have been defined by balancing the public interest in the confidentiality of grand jury proceedings against the public interest in disclosure in a particular context.[153] In some cases such as disclosure to a second grand jury, the rule permits disclosure without court approval; in other cases such as disclosure to a civil litigant, the rule requires court approval after balancing the conflicting interests represented in a particular request for disclosure.

The areas beyond the cloak of grand jury secrecy may include instances where: (1) the individual with the information is not bound to maintain the grand jury's secrets; (2) disclosure does not constitute disclosure of "matters occurring before the grand jury"; (3) subsequent use of the information presented to the grand jury is not a "disclosure;" (4) the disclosure is to an attorney for the government or a government employee for use in the performance of the attorney's duties; (5) disclosure is "directed by the court preliminary to or in connection with a judicial proceeding;" (6) a defendant seeks to dismiss an indictment because of grand jury irregularities; (7) an attorney for the government discloses the information to another grand jury; (8) disclosed to state officials for purposes of enforcing state law; (9) disclosure is expressly permitted by statute; and (10) continued secrecy would be inconsistent with history of the grand jury's relationship with the court and of the common law origins of the rule.

Those Who Need Not Keep the Grand Jury's Secrets

Rule 6 expressly declares that "[n]o obligation of secrecy may be imposed on any person except in accordance with" its provisions,[154] and only proscribes disclosures by members of the grand jury, its court reporters and interpreters, the attorney for the government, and any personnel to whom grand jury matters are disclosed so that they may assist the attorney for the government.

Thus, a grand jury witness may ordinarily disclose his or her grand jury testimony,[155] and those not listed in Rule 6 generally need not keep the grand jury's secrets even if they learned of the matter from someone bound by the rule of secrecy.[156]

Matters

Grand jury secrecy shrouds "matter[s] occurring before the grand jury."[157] It does not ordinarily bar disclosure of information because the information might be presented to the grand jury at some time in the future.[158] The rule protects the workings of the grand jury not the grist for its mill. The fact of disclosure to the grand jury, rather than the information disclosed, is the object of protection, but the two are not always easily separated. Clearly, grand jury secrecy does not bar disclosure of information previously presented to a grand jury but sought for an unrelated purpose by a requester unaware of its earlier presentation. On the other hand, it does cover instances where information is sought because it has been presented to the grand jury. In between, the distinctions become more difficult and the cases do not reflect a single approach.[159]

Rule 6(e) also shields ancillary proceedings and records to avoid frustration of its purpose during the course of litigation concerning the proper scope of the rule,[160] but the Rule "requires that records, orders, and subpoenas relating to grand-jury proceedings remain sealed only to the extent and as long as necessary to prevent the unauthorized disclosure of such matters. . . [W]hen once-secret grand jury material becomes sufficiently widely known, it may lose its character as Rule 6(e) material."[161]

Disclosure

The rule contemplates disclosure of matters occurring before the grand jury under a number of circumstances. Some require court approval; others do not.

Government Attorneys and Employees

Government attorneys and other employees may benefit from access to matters occurring before the grand jury in a number of instances. For example, grand jury secrecy does not prevent a government attorney (who acquired information and prepared documents while assisting a grand jury) from reviewing and using the information and documents, without disclosing them to anyone else, in preparation for civil litigation.[162]

Moreover, disclosure to government attorneys and employees assisting the grand jury without court approval is likewise possible under 6(e)(3)(A).[163] The Supreme Court has made it clear that such disclosures are limited to attorneys and employees assisting in the criminal process which is the focus of the grand jury's inquiry.[164] Grand jury material may be disclosed without court approval under (3)(A) to enable state police officers to assist a federal grand jury investigation, but apparently not private contractors.[165]

The rule, however, permits disclosure of grand jury evidence of certain foreign and terrorist criminal activities to various law enforcement officials without prior judicial approval. More specifically, rule 6(e)(3)(D) authorizes disclosure of grand jury information concerning foreign nations, their agents and activities to federal, state, local, tribal and foreign officials without court approval, although the court must be notified after the fact.[166]

Judicial Proceedings

Rule 6(e)(3)(E)(i) permits court approved disclosure of grand jury matters "preliminarily to or in connection with a judicial proceeding."[167] Historically, the courts concluded, with some dissent, that the exception applied not only to the trial which followed the grand jury's investigation but to variety of proceedings range from state bar and police disciplinary investigations,[168] to parole hearings,[169] state criminal investigations,[170] Congressional inquiries,[171] federal administrative proceedings,[172] civil litigation,[173] and other grand jury investigations.[174] In *United States v. Baggot*, however, the Supreme Court provide guidance as to when disclosure might be considered "preliminarily to or in connection with" an appropriate proceeding and some indication of what kinds of proceedings might be considered "judicial":

> [T]he term "in connection with," in (C)(i) . . . refer[s] to a judicial proceeding already pending, while "preliminary to" refers to one not yet initiated. . . . The "judicial proceeding" language . . . reflects a judgment that not every beneficial purpose, or even every valid governmental purpose, is an appropriate reason for breaching grand jury secrecy. Rather, the rule contemplates only uses related fairly directly to some identifiable litigation, pending or anticipated. Thus, it is not enough to show that some litigation may emerge form the matter in which the material is to be used, or even that litigation is factually likely to emerge. The focus is on the *actual* use to be made of the material. If the primary purpose of disclosure is not to assist in preparation or conduct of a judicial proceeding, disclosure under (C)(i) is not permitted. 463 U.S. 476, 479-80 (1983)(emphasis of the Court).

Using this criterion, *Baggot* concluded that disclosure of grand jury matter to the government for purposes of a tax audit, after which any tax liability could be enforced nonjudicially, could not be considered "preliminary to or in connection with a judicial proceeding" and thus could not be permitted under (C)(i).[175]

Baggot found it unnecessary to address "the knotty question of what, if any, sorts of proceedings other than the garden-variety civil actions or criminal prosecutions might qualify as judicial proceedings under (C)(i)."[176] The case's description of disclosures in an administrative context, however, hardly supports the notion that "judicial proceedings" include those before administrative tribunals.[177]

Particularized Need

Court approved disclosures require "a strong showing of particularized need."[178] Petitioners seeking disclosure "must show that the material they seek is needed to avoid a possible injustice in another judicial proceeding, that the need for disclosure is greater than the need for continued secrecy, and that their request is structured to cover only material so needed."[179]

Since any examination begins with a preference for preservation of the grand jury's secrets, the particularized need requirement cannot be satisfied simply by demonstrating that the information sought would be relevant or useful or that acquiring it from the grand jury rather than from some other available source would be more convenient.[180]

While the test remains the same whether the government or a private party seeks disclosure,[181] "the concerns that underlie the policy of grand jury secrecy are implicated to a much lesser extent when the disclosure merely involves government attorneys."[182]

In the balance to be struck in the process of determining whether "the need for disclosure is greater than the need for continued secrecy,"[183] the district court enjoys discretion to judge each case on its own facts,[184] but some general trends seem to have developed.

The need to shield the grand jury's activities from public display is less compelling once it has completed its inquiries and been discharged,[185] especially if the resulting criminal proceedings have also been concluded.[186] Of course, there must still be a counterbalancing demonstration of need,[187] a requirement that becomes more difficult if the grand jury witnesses whose testimony is be disclosed still run the risk of retaliation.[188]

"Courts have consistently distinguished the requests for documents generated independent of the grand jury investigation from the request for grand jury minutes or witness transcripts reasoning that the degree of exposure of the grand jury process inherent in the revelation of subpoenaed documents is lesser than the degree of disclosure attributable to publication of witness transcripts."[189]

Moreover, the courts seem responsive to requests to disclose matters occurring before the grand jury in order to resolve some specific inconsistency in the testimony of a witness or to refresh a witness's collection during the course of a trial.[190] In the same vein, they are more disposed to the interests supporting disclosure if the petitioner's opponent already enjoys the benefit of the information sought.[191]

Defendant's Motion to Dismiss[192]

Rule 6(e)(3)(E)(ii) permits court approved disclosure upon a defendant's request "showing grounds may exist for a motion to dismiss the indictment because of matters occurring before the grand jury," and upon a showing of particularized need.[193]

Second Grand Jury[194]

Grand jury matters may be disclosed to another federal grand jury without court approval under Rule 6(e)(3)(C). Prior to enactment of this part of the Rule, disclosure to another federal grand jury was possible upon a showing of particularized need "preliminary to or in connection with a judicial proceeding" under (E)(i). Neither particularized need nor court approval are apparently any longer required and disclosure is permitted whether the two panels are sitting within the same district or not.[195]

State, Military, or Foreign Law Enforcement[196]

Where the grand jury matters may show evidence of a violation of state law, the attorney for the government may petition the court for disclosure to state, military, or foreign enforcement authorities under Rule 6(e)(3)(E)(iii), (iv), (v).[197]

Express Authority under Statute or Other Rule

A criminal defendant is entitled to inspect and copy that portion of the transcript of his or her own testimony before a grand jury which relates to a crime with which he or she has been charged.[198] And, under the Jencks Act, after a witness has testified against a defendant at trial, the defendant is entitled to request and receive a copy of the witness' relevant grand jury testimony.[199]

Congress has expressly authorized the disclosure of grand jury matters in connection with enforcement of some of the banking laws.[200] In the case of civil penalties for bank fraud, false statements and embezzlement and civil forfeiture for money laundering, the attorney for the government may receive information concerning grand jury matters from the attorney who assisted the grand jury or any of his or her assistants. Bank regulatory agency personnel may receive grand jury information concerning such misconduct upon a motion by the government showing substantial need.

But Congress's intent to breach the general rule of secrecy must be clear. Thus the disclosure of grand jury matters is not authorized by those provisions of the Clayton Act which in certain antitrust instances compel the United States Attorney General to provide state Attorneys General with "any investigative files or other materials which are or may be relevant or material" to a cause action under the Act.[201]

Consistence with the Historical Dimensions of Grand Jury Secrecy

Several courts, conscious of a responsibility over the grand jury subpoenas and indictments and of the common law origins of Rule 6(e), have permitted or asserted that under the proper circumstances they would permit disclosure without reference to any particular express exception within Rule 6(e) or elsewhere.[202] Others, for much the same reasons, have noted that under the appropriate circumstances, a court might restrict disclosure of grand jury matters even in instances where Rule 6(e) would ordinarily permit disclosure.[203]

Enforcement of Grand Jury Secrecy

"A knowing violation of Rule 6 . . . may be punished as a contempt of court."[204] Since the Rule speaks of punishment, it might be fair to assume that it contemplates criminal contempt. And it does, but the courts have also held that violations of grand jury secrecy may subject offenders to civil contempt and to the injunctive power of the court.[205] Government employees and members of the bar who improperly disclose the grand jury's secrets may be subject to disciplinary proceedings.[206] Under some circumstances, improper disclosure of grand jury matters may also violate the obstruction of justice provisions of 18 U.S.C. 1503 (corruptly impeding or endeavoring to impede the administration of justice in connection with a judicial proceeding).[207]

FINAL GRAND JURY ACTION

There are four possible outcomes of convening a grand jury – (1) indictment, (2) a vote not to indict, to find ""no bill"" or "no true bill", or to endorse the indictment "ignoramus", (3) discharge or expiration without any action, (4) submission of a report to the court.

Indictment

In an indictment the grand jury accuses a designated person with a specific crime. It contains a "plain, concise and definite written statement of the essential facts constituting the offense charged" and bears the signature of the attorney for the government, and of the grand jury foreperson.[208] The "constitution requirements for an indictment [are], first, that it contains the elements of the offense charged and fairly informs a defendant of the charge against which he must defend, and second, that it enables him to plead an acquittal or conviction in bar of future prosecutions for the same offense."[209]

Every defendant to be tried for a federal capital or "otherwise infamous crime" has a constitutional right to demand that the process begin only after the concurrence of twelve of his or her fellow citizens reflected in an indictment.[210] It is a right, however, which the defendant may waive in noncapital cases and be charged under an information filed by the prosecutor without grand jury involvement.[211] Misdemeanors may, but need not, be tried by indictment.[212]

The grand jury may indict only upon the vote of twelve of its members,[213] and upon its conclusion that there is probable cause to believe that the accused committed the crime charged.[214]

Defendants have urged dismissal of their indictments based upon a wide array of alleged grand jury irregularities. They are rarely successful. The irregularities which warrant dismissal are few and the obstacles which must be overcome to establish them substantial.

The courts are most hospitable to dismissal motions predicated upon constitutional violations. Thus, indictments returned by grand jury panels whose selection has been tainted by racial or sexual discrimination will be dismissed.[215] The courts will likewise dismiss indictments which charge a defendant on basis of his or her immunized testimony taken pursuant to an order entered in lieu of his or her Fifth Amendment self-incrimination privilege;[216] which are defective for failure to state an offense contrary to the Fifth Amendment right of indictment before trial for a felony;[217] which are tainted by violations of the Speech or Debate privilege,[218] of the right of the accused to counsel of his choice;[219] which are based *solely* on evidence secured in violation of the Fourth Amendment;[220] or which charge violation of a statute that is unconstitutional on its face.[221]

They will also dismiss indictments in the name of due process where the prosecution sought indictment selectively for constitutionally impermissible reasons;[222] or for reasons of vindictive retaliation;[223] where the prosecution has secured the indictment through outrageous conduct which shocks the conscience of the court;[224] where the prosecution has unjustifiably delayed seeking an indictment to the detriment of the defendant;[225] where the government knowingly secures the indictment through the presentation of false or perjured testimony;[226] or where a witness is called before the grand jury for the sole purpose of building perjury prosecution against the witness.[227]

In the absence of one of these rarely found causes for constitutional challenge, a facially valid indictment returned by a legally constituted grand jury is almost uniformly immune from dismissal.[228] "*Bank of Nova Scotia v. United States*, [however,] makes it clear that the supervisory power can be used to dismiss an indictment because of misconduct before the grand jury, at least where the misconduct amounts to a violation of one of those few, clear rules which were carefully drafted and approved by this Court and by Congress to ensure the integrity of the grand jury functions."[229]

Bank of Nova Scotia also makes it clear, nevertheless, that such supervisory authority to dismiss an indictment is only appropriately exercised where "'it is established that the violations substantially influenced the grand jury's decision to indict' or if there is 'grave doubt' that the decision was free from such substantial influence."[230] If the error is harmless the indictment may not be dismissed;[231] "a district court may not dismiss an indictment for errors in grand jury proceedings unless such errors prejudiced the defendants."[232] Timing is also important. After a trial jury has found sufficient evidence to convict a defendant, a claim of prejudice based on grand jury irregularities may lose must of its force.[233]

Finally, the supervisory power to dismiss an indictment does not appear to extend beyond those areas where it is reinforced by the Constitution, statute or rule.[234] As a consequence of these limitations, indictments will not ordinarily be dismissed because:

- the prosecutor failed to present evidence favorable to the defendant;[235]
- the prosecutor failed to properly instruct the panel on applicable law;[236]
- the prosecutor failed to advise the witness that he was a target of the investigation contrary to a suggestion in United States Attorney's Manual[237]
- the accused was called to testify before the grand jury when the prosecutor was aware the witness would invoke his privilege against self-incrimination;[238]
- the prosecutor presented the grand jury with a signed indictment for its consideration and approval or rejection;[239]
- of inflammatory press coverage proximate to the grand jury's inquiry;[240]
- of a breached grand jury secrecy;[241]
- of the presence of unauthorized individuals while the grand jury conducted its business;[242]
- of the presentation of hearsay evidence;[243]
- of the presentation of inaccurate, unreliable, misleading, or false evidence;[244]
- of the presentation of illegal obtained evidence;[245]
- of the presentation of evidence secured in violation of the Fourth Amendment;[246]

- of the presentation of evidence secured by intrusion into the attorney-client relationship;[247]
- of the presentation of evidence secured in violation of the Constitution's speech and debate clause;[248] or
- no twelve grand jurors heard all the evidence upon which the indictment was based.[249]

In addition to dismissal of the indictment at the request of the accused, the government may move for dismissal of the indictment under Rule 48(a). Although the rule requires "leave of court," prosecutorial discretion is vested in the executive and the court cannot effectively compel prosecution. The authority of the courts to deny dismissal is therefore limited to instances where dismissal would be "clearly contrary to manifest public interest."[250] In most instances, dismissal at the government's behest is without prejudice, and the prosecutor may seek to reindict for the same offense as long as neither speedy trial nor the double jeopardy clause pose a bar.[251]

Refusal to Indict

The decision to indict rests with the grand jury. It may indict in the face of probable cause, but it need not; it cannot be required to indict nor punished for failing to do so.[252] On the other hand, the prosecution is free to resubmit a matter for reconsideration by the same grand jury or by a subsequent panel and a grand jury panel is free to reexamine a matter notwithstanding the prior results of its own deliberations or those of another panel.[253] Moreover, the defendant will not be heard to complain that the panel was not informed of their prerogative to decline to indict even if presented with probable cause.[254]

Reports[255]

The law regarding the last alternative available to the grand jury, the authority to send forward "reports" or "presentments," is somewhat obscure. At common law "indictments" were returned by the grand jury based upon evidence presented to the grand jury, while "presentments" were "the notice taken by the grand jury of any offense from their own knowledge or observation, without any bill of indictment laid before them at the suit of the king."[256] It is clear that in the limited case of the special grand juries convened under 18 U.S.C. 3331-3334, the grand jury has statutory authority to report on organized crime.[257] Most federal grand jury panels, however, have no express authority to issue reports.

They nevertheless appear to have common law authority to prepare reports, at least under some circumstances.[258] The district court which empanels the grand jury receives such communications and enjoys the discretion to determine the extent to which the reports should be sealed, expunged or disclosed. Some of the factors considered in making that determination include: "whether the report describes general community conditions or whether it refers to identifiable individuals; whether the individuals are mentioned in public or private capacities; the public interest in the contents of the report balanced against the harm to the individuals named; the availability and efficacy of remedies; whether the conduct described is indictable;"[259] and whether the report intrudes upon the prerogatives of state and local governments.[260]

Discharge

The court has the power to discharge a grand jury panel at any time within its term for any reason it sees fit.[261] The court's authority to discharge a panel, quash its subpoenas, seal or expunge its reports or dismiss its indictments afford a check on "runaway" grand jury panels.[262]

References

Books and Articles

Antell, *Modern Grand Jury: Benighted Supergovernment*, 51 American Bar Association Journal 153 (1965)

Arenella, *Reforming the Federal Grand Jury and the State Preliminary Hearing to Prevent Conviction Without Adjudication*, 78 Michigan Law Review 463 (1980)

Bartlett, *Defendants' Right to an Unbiased Federal Grand Jury*, 47 Boston University Law Review 551 (1967)

Beale, Bryson, Felman and Elston, Grand Jury Law and Practice (1998 and 2007-2008 Supp.)

Boudin, *Federal Grand Jury*, 61 Georgetown Law Journal 1 (1973)

Boyle, *The Material Witness Statute Post September 11: Why It Should Not Include Grand Jury Witnesses*, 48 NEW YORK LAW SCHOOL LAW REVIEW 12 (2003).

Brenner and Shaw, FEDERAL GRAND JURY: A GUIDE TO LAW AND PRACTICE (2d ed. 2006)

Brenner, *Is the Grand Jury Worth Keeping?* 81 JUDICATURE 190 (1998)

Brown, *The Witness and Grand Jury Secrecy*, 11 AMERICAN JOURNAL OF CRIMINAL LAW 169 (1983)

Calkins, *Abolition of the Grand Jury Indictment in Illinois*, 1966 UNIVERSITY OF ILLINOIS LAW FORUM 423 *Grand Jury Secrecy*, 63 MICHIGAN LAW REVIEW 455 (1965)

Campbell, *Eliminate the Grand Jury*, 64 JOURNAL OF CRIMINAL LAW and CRIMINOLOGY 174 (1973)

Cassidy, *Toward a More Independent Grand Jury: Recasting and Enforcing the Prosecutor's Duty to Disclose Exculpatory Evidence*, 13 GEORGETOWN JOURNAL OF LEGAL ETHICS 361 (2000)

Clark, THE GRAND JURY: USE AND ABUSE OF POLITICAL POWER (1975)

Collins, *And the Walls Came Tumbling Down: Sharing Grand Jury Information with the Intelligence Community Under the USA PATRIOT Act*, 39 AMERICAN CRIMINAL LAW REVIEW 1261 (2002)

Decker, *Legislating New Federalism: The Call for Grand Jury Reform in the States*, 58 OKLAHOMA LAW REVIEW 341 (2005)

Dession, *From Indictment to Information — Implications of the Shift*, 42 YALE LAW JOURNAL 163 (1932)

Dession and Cohn, *The Inquisitorial Functions of Grand Juries*, 41 YALE LAW JOURNAL 687 (1932)

Deutsch, *The Improper Use of the Federal Grand Jury: An Instrument of Political Activists*, 75 JOURNAL OF CRIMINAL LAW and CRIMINOLOGY 1159 (1984)

Diamond, FEDERAL GRAND JURY PRACTICE AND PROCEDURE (1997) Edwards, THE GRAND JURY (1906)

Farrell, *An Overview of How Grand Juries Operate*, 31 CHAMPION 26 (July, 2007)

Field, *Federal History, Functions, Duties and Powers of Federal Grand Juries*, 20 PITTSBURGH LEGAL JOURNAL 22 (1982)

Frankel and Naftalis, THE GRAND JURY: AN INSTITUTION ON TRIAL (1977)

Gelber, *A Reappraisal of the Grand Jury Concept*, 60 JOURNAL OF CRIMINAL LAW, CRIMINOLOGY and POLICE SCIENCE 24 (1969)

Gerstein and Robinson, *Remedy for the Grand Jury: Retain But Reform*, 64 AMERICAN BAR ASSOCIATION JOURNAL 337 (1978)

Glanzer and Taskier, *Attorneys Before the Grand Jury: Assertion of the Attorney-Client Privilege to Protect a Client's Identity*, 75 JOURNAL OF CRIMINAL LAW and CRIMINOLOGY 1070 (1984)

Glynn, *The Grand Jury Report as an Infringement of Private Rights*, 23 HASTINGS LAW JOURNAL 561 (1972)

Hall, *Analysis of Criticism of the Grand Jury*, 22 JOURNAL OF CRIMINAL LAW and CRIMINOLOGY 692 (1932)

Henning, *Prosecutorial Misconduct in Grand Jury Investigations*, 51 SOUTH CAROLINA LAW REVIEW 1 (1999)

Hixson, *Bringing Down the Curtain on the Absurd Drama of Entrance and Exists — Witness Representation in the Grand Jury Room*, 15 AMERICAN CRIMINAL LAW REVIEW 307 (1978)

Hughes, *Administrative Subpoenas and the Grand Jury: Converging Streams of Criminal and Civil Compulsory Process*, 47 VANDERBILT LAW REVIEW 573 (1994)

Kadish, *Behind the Locked Door of an American Grand Jury: Its History, Its Secrecy, and Its Process*, 24 FLORIDA STATE UNIVERSITY LAW REVIEW 1 (1996)

Kuckes, *The Democratic Prosecutor: Explaining the Constitutional Function of the Federal Grand Jury*, 94 GEORGETOWN LAW JOURNAL 1265 (2006) *The Useful, Dangerous Fiction of Grand Jury Independence*, 41 AMERICAN CRIMINAL LAW REVIEW 1 (2004)

Kuh, *Grand Jury "Presentment": Foul Blow or Fair Play?* 55 COLUMBIA LAW REVIEW 1103 (1955)

Leipold, *Why Grand Juries Do Not (and Cannot) Protect the Accused*, 80 CORNELL LAW REVIEW 260 (1995)

Misner, *In Partial Praise of* Boyd: *The Grand Jury as Catalyst for Fourth Amendment Change*, 29 ARIZONA STATE LAW JOURNAL 805 (1997)

Morse, *A Survey of the Grand Jury System*, 10 OREGON LAW REVIEW 101 (1931)

Orfield, *Federal Grand Jury*, 22 FEDERAL RULES DECISIONS 343 (1958)

Poulin, *Supervision of the Grand Jury: Who Watches the Guardian?*, 68 WASHINGTON UNIVERSITY LAW QUARTERLY 885 (1990)

Richman, *Grand Jury Secrecy: Plugging the Leaks in the an Empty Bucket*, 36 AMERICAN CRIMINAL LAW REVIEW 339 (1999)

Roots, *If It's Not a Runaway, It's Not a Real Grand Jury*, 33 CREIGHTON LAW REVIEW 821 (2000)

Schneider, *The Grand Jury: Powers, Procedures and Problems*, 9 COLUMBIA JOURNAL OF LAW and SOCIAL PROBLEMS 681 (1973)

Schwartz, *Demythologizing the Historic Role of the Grand Jury*, 10 AMERICAN CRIMINAL LAW REVIEW 701 (1972)

Shaw, *The USA PATRIOT Act of 2001, the Intelligence Reform and Terrorism Prevention Act of 2004, and the False Dichotomy Between Protecting National Security and Preserving Grand Jury Secrecy*, 35 SETON HALL LAW REVIEW 495 (2005)

Silbert, *Defense Counsel in the Grand Jury – The Answer to the White Collar Criminal's Prayers*, 15 AMERICAN CRIMINAL LAW REVIEW 293 (1978)

Simmons, *Re-examining the Grand Jury: Is There Room for Democracy in the Criminal Justice System?* 82 BOSTON UNIVERSITY LAW REVIEW 1 (2002)

Stern, *Revealing Misconduct by Public Officials Through Grand Jury Reports*, 136 UNIVERSITY OF PENNSYLVANIA LAW REVIEW 73 (1987)

Sullivan and Bachman, *If It Ain't Broke, Don't Fix It: Why the Grand Jury's Accusatory Function*

Should Not Be Changed, 75 JOURNAL OF CRIMINAL LAW and CRIMINOLOGY 1047 (1984)

Tigar and Levy, *Grand Jury as the New Inquisition*, 50 MICHIGAN STATE BAR JOURNAL 693 (1971)

Trichter and Lewis, *The Grand Jury, Putative Grand Jury Witnesses and the Right to Limited Counsel — A Historical Overview and Modest Proposal*, 20 SOUTH TEXAS LAW JOURNAL 81 (1979)

United States Department of Justice, FEDERAL GRAND JURY PRACTICE (Aug. 2000)

United States House of Representatives, *Constitutional Rights and the Grand Jury: Hearing Before the Subcomm. on the Constitution of the House Comm. on the Judiciary*, 106th Cong., 2d Sess. (2000) (at www.house.gov/judiciary/constitution)

______, *Federal Grand Jury: Hearings Before the Subcomm. on Immigration, Citizenship, and International Law of the House Comm. on the Judiciary*, 94th Cong., 2d Sess. (1976)

______, *Grand Jury Reform: Hearings Before the Subcomm. on Immigration, Citizenship, and International Law of the House Comm. on the Judiciary*, 95th Cong., 1st Sess. (1977)

______, *Grand Jury Reform: Hearings Before the Subcomm. on Criminal Justice of the House Comm. on the Judiciary*, 99th Cong., 1st and 2d Sess. (1986)

______, *Grand Jury Reform: Hearings Before the Subcomm. on Criminal Justice of the House Comm. on the Judiciary*, 100th Cong., 1st Sess. (1987)

______, *Grand Jury Venue – Northern District of Texas: Hearings Before Subcomm. No. 1 of the House Comm. on the Judiciary*, 93d Cong., 1st Sess. (1973)

______, *Proposed Amendments to the Federal Rules of Criminal Procedure: Hearings Before the Subcomm. on Criminal Justice of the House Comm. on the Judiciary*, 95th Cong., 1st Sess. (1977)

United States Senate, *The Grand Jury Reform Act of 1978: Hearings Before the Subcomm. on Administrative Practice and Procedure of the Senate Comm. on the Judiciary*, 95th Cong., 2d Sess. (1978)

Vaira, *The Role of the Prosecutor Inside the Grand Jury Room: Where Is the Foul Line?* 75 JOURNAL OF CRIMINAL LAW and CRIMINOLOGY 1129 (1984)

Watts, *Grand Jury: Sleeping Watchdog or Expensive Antique?* 37 NORTH CAROLINA LAW REVIEW 290 (1959)

Whyte, *Is the Grand Jury Necessary?* 45 VIRGINIA LAW REVIEW 461 (1959)

Wright, FEDERAL PRACTICE AND PROCEDURE: CRIMINAL 3D (1999)

Younger, THE PEOPLES PANEL: THE GRAND JURY IN THE UNITED STATES, 1634-1941 (1963)

Zacharias, *A Critical Look at Rules Governing Grand Jury Subpoenas of Attorneys*, 76 MINNESOTA LAW REVIEW 917 (1992)

Zwerling, *Federal Grand Juries v. Attorney Independence and the Attorney-Client Privilege*, 27 HASTINGS LAW JOURNAL 1263 (1976)

Notes and Comments

Adding Bite to the Watchdog's Bark: Reforming the California Civil Grand Jury System, 28 PACIFIC LAW JOURNAL 1115 (1997).

Availability of Civil Remedies Under the Grand Jury Secrecy Rule, 47 CATHOLIC UNIVERSITY LAW REVIEW 237 (1997)

A Critical Appraisal of the Justice Department Guidelines for Grand Jury Subpoenas Issued to Defense Attorneys, 1986 DUKE LAW JOURNAL 145

The Emasculation of Compelled Testimony: Battling the Effects of Judicially Imposed Limitations on Grand Jury Investigations of Terrorism and Other Ideological Crimes, 70 SOUTHERN CALIFORNIA LAW REVIEW 473 (1997)

Extension of Grand Jury Term Under 18 U.S.C.S. §3331 or Under Rule 6(g) of Federal Rules of Criminal Procedure, as Amended in 1983, 98 ALR FED 901

Federal Rule of Criminal Procedure 6(e): Criminal or Civil Contempt for Violations of Grand Jury Secrecy? 12 WESTERN NEW ENGLAND LAW REVIEW 245 (1990)

Federal Rule of Criminal Procedure 6(e) and the Disclosure of Documents Reviewed by a Grand Jury, 57 UNIVERSITY OF CHICAGO LAW REVIEW 221 (1990)

Fourth Amendment — The Presumption of Reasonableness of a Subpoena Duces Tecum Issued by a Grand Jury, 82 JOURNAL OF CRIMINAL LAW and CRIMINOLOGY 829 (1992)

The Grand Jury as an Investigating Body, 74 HARVARD LAW REVIEW 590 (1961)

The Grand Jury Report as an Infringement on Private Rights, 23 HASTINGS LAW JOURNAL 561 (1972)

Indianhead Poker in the Grand Jury Room: Prosecutorial Suppression of Exculpatory Evidence, 28 VALPARISO UNIVERSITY LAW REVIEW 1377 (1994)

Nineteenth Survey of White Collar Crime: Procedural Issues, 41 AMERICAN CRIMINAL LAW REVIEW 973 (2004)

Preserving Justice and Preventing Prejudice: Requiring Disclosure of Substantial Exculpatory Evidence to the Grand Jury, 39 AMERICAN CRIMINAL LAW REVIEW 171 (2002)

Return to Certainty: Why Grand Jury Subpoenas Should Supersede Civil Protective Orders, 10 SUFFOLK JOURNAL OF TRIAL AND APPELLATE ADVOCACY 43 (2005)

Reviving Federal Grand Jury Presentments, 103 YALE LAW JOURNAL 1333 (1994)

Right of Party in Civil Action to Obtain Disclosure, Under Rule 6(e)(3)(C)(i) of the Federal Rules of Criminal Procedure, of Matters Occurring Before Grand Jury, 71 ALR FED 10

The Right to Grand Jury Indictment, 26 AMERICAN CRIMINAL LAW REVIEW 1457 (1989)

Should a Grand Jury Subpoena Override a District Court's Protective Order? 64 UNIVERSITY OF CHICAGO LAW REVIEW 317 (1997)

Thirty-Fifth Annual Review of Criminal Procedure: Grand Jury, 35 GEORGETOWN LAW JOURNAL ANNUAL REVIEW CRIMINAL PROCEDURE 226 (2006)

What Actions of the United states Attorney Constitute Usurpation of Authority of Federal Grand Jury, Thus Warranting Exclusion of Evidence Obtained Thereby, 65 ALR FED 957

What Do You Do With a Runaway Grand Jury? A Discussion of the Problems and Possibilities Opened Up by the Rocky Flats Grand Jury Investigation, 71 SOUTHERN CALIFORNIA LAW REVIEW 617 (1998).

REFERENCES

[1] United States v. R. Enterprises, Inc., 498 U.S. 292, 297 (1991).

[2] United States v. Cox, 342 F.2d 167, 186 n.1 (5th Cir. 1965)(Wisdom, J., concurring), quoting American Bar Association, FEDERAL GRAND JURY HANDBOOK 8 (1959) (reprinted in Federal Grand Jury: Hearings Before the Subcomm. on Immigration, Citizenship, and International Law of the House Comm. on the Judiciary, 94th Cong., 2d Sess. 277, 283 (1976)).

[3] "No person shall be held to answer for a capital, or otherwise infamous crime, unless on a presentment or indictment of a grand jury. . . ." U.S. Const. Amend. V. A defendant is free to waive grand jury indictment for any crime that does not carry the death penalty; and the government may prosecute misdemeanors and other minor federal crimes by either by indictment or by information, F.R.Crim.P. 7.

[4] Most commentators, after making reference to earlier similar institutions in ancient Greece, Rome, Scandinavia, Normandy and/or among the Saxons, trace the emergence of the modern grand jury to the issuance of the Assize of Clarendon by Henry II in 1166, 1 Stephen, A HISTORY OF THE CRIMINAL LAW OF ENGLAND, 251-52 (1883); 1 Holdsworth, HISTORY OF ENGLISH LAW, 147-48 (1903); Stubbs, SELECT CHARTERS AND OTHER ILLUSTRATIONS OF ENGLISH CONSTITUTIONAL HISTORY, 143 (1888); 2 Pollack and Maitland, HISTORY OF ENGLISH LAW, 642 (1923); Plucknett, A CONCISE HISTORY OF THE COMMON LAW 112 (1956); Schwartz, Demythologizing the Historic Role of the Grand Jury, 10 AMERICAN CRIMINAL LAW REVIEW 701, 703 (1972); Boudin, The Federal Grand Jury, 61 GEORGETOWN LAW JOURNAL 1 (1972); Kadish, Behind the Locked Door of an American Grand Jury: Its History, Its Secrecy, and Its Process, 24 FLORIDA STATE UNIVERSITY LAW REVIEW 1, 5-6 (1996). In the Assize of Clarendon and the later Assize of Northampton (1176), "twelve

knights of the hundred or, if there are no knights, . . . twelve free and lawful men, . . . and . . . four men from each township of the hundred" were assembled and "by their oath" identified from their own knowledge those reputed to have committed crimes. Plucknett, supra at 112; 3 Stephen, supra at 251; 1 Holdsworth, supra at 147. "Assize" literally means "to sit together" and comes from the practice of gathering several knights or men of high repute to sit together and resolve some dispute or other legal matter from their own investigations or knowledge. Later the term was used (a) to designate the decree or statute that ordered the group to assemble, (b) to refer to the assemblage itself, and finally (c) to identify the court, time or place where the trial judges assembled throughout the country side to hear cases. BLACK'S LAW DICTIONARY, 120-21 (1990).

[5] Plucknett, supra at 112. At common law, anyone convicted and "attained" for treason or felony forfeited all his land and goods to the Crown, 4 Blackstone, COMMENTARIES 376-81 (1813 ed.); 1 Hale, HISTORY OF PLEAS OF THE CROWN, 354-67 (1778 ed.).

[6] Story, COMMENTARIES ON THE CONSTITUTION OF THE UNITED STATES, 658 (1833 ed.); United States v. Williams, 504 U.S. 36, 47-8 (1992)("In fact the whole theory of [the grand jury's] function is that it belongs to no branch of the institutional Government, serving as a kind of buffer or referee between the Government and the people").

[7] The Fifth Amendment right to grand jury indictment is not binding upon the states, Hurtado v. California, 110 U.S. 516 (1884); Gautt v. Lewis, 489 F.3d 993, 1103 n.10 (9th Cir. 2007); Goodrich v. Hall, 448 F.3d 45, 49 (1st Cir. 2006); Williams v. Haviland, 467 F.3d 527, 531 (6th Cir. 2006); Lanfranco v. Murray, 313 F.3d 112, 118 (2d Cir. 2002); (Freeman v. City of Dallas, 242 F.3d 642, 667 (5th Cir. 2001); Holman v. Gilmore, 126 F.3d 876, 884 (7th Cir. 1997); Cooksey v. Delo, 94 F.3d 1214, 1217 (8th Cir. 1996); Minner v. Kerby, 30 F.3d 1311, 1318 (10th Cir. 1994);cf., Rose v. Mitchell, 443 U.S. 545, 557 n.7 (1979).

[8] Ala. Const.I, §8; Ala.R.Crim.P. 2.1, 2.2(e); Ariz. Const. Art.II, §30; Ariz.R.Crim.P. 2.2; Ark. Const. Amend. 21, §1; Cal. Const. Art.I, §14, Cal.Penal Code §737; Colo. Const. Art.II, §8, Colo.Rev.Stat. §16-5-101; Conn. Gen.Laws Ann. §§54-45, 54-46; Fla. Const. Art. I, §15; Hawaii Const. Art.I, §10; Hawaii Rev.Stat.Ann. §801-1; Idaho Const. Art.I, §8; Ill. Const. Art.I, §7, Ill. Comp.Stat.Ann. ch.725

§5/111-2; Ind.Stat. Ann. §35-34-1-1; Iowa R. Crim.P. 2.4; Kan.Stat.Ann. §22-3201; La. Const. Art.I, §15; Md.Ann.Code, Crim.P. §1-101; Mich. Comp.Laws Ann. §767.1; Minn.R.Crim.P. 17.01; Mo. Const. Art.I, §17; Mont. Const. Art.II, §20, Mont.Code Ann. §46-11-101; Neb. Const. Bill of Rts. §10; Neb.Rev.Stat. §29-1601; Nev. Const. Art.I, §8; N.M. Const. Art.II, §14; N.D. R.Crim.P. 7; Okla. Const. Art.II, §17; Ore. Const. Art.VII, §5; R.I. Const. Art. I, §7; S.D. Const. Art.VI, §10; S.D.Comp.Laws Ann. §23A-6-1; Utah Const. Art.I, §13; Vt.R.Crim.P. 7; Wash. Const. Art.I, §25; Wis.Stat. Ann. §967.05; Wyo. Const. Art.I, §13, Wyo.R.Crim.P. 3. Several states do continue to recognize a right to grand jury indictment in felony cases, Alaska Const. Art. I, §8; Del. Const. Art. I, §8; Ga.Code Ann. §§17-7-70; Ky. Bill of Rts. §12; Me.Const. Art.I, §7; Mass.Gen.Laws Ann. ch. 263, §4; Miss. Const. Art.III, §27; N.H.Rev.Stat.Ann. §601:1; N.J. Const. Art.I, ¶8; N.Y. Const. Art. I, §6; N.C. Const. Art. I, §22; Ohio Const. Art.I, § 10; Pa.Const. Art.I, §10; S.C. Const. Art. I, §11; Tenn. Const. Art. I, §14; Tex. Const. Art. I, §10; Va.Code §§19.2-216, 19.2-217; W.Va. Const. Art. III, §4. And a few others require it in cases punishable by death or life imprisonment, Ala.Const. I, §8; Conn. Gen.Laws Ann. §54-45 (offenses punishable by death or life imprisonment committed prior to May 26, 1983); Fla. Const. Art. I, §15; La. Const. Art.I, §15; R.I. Const. Art. I. §7.

[9] "The obituary of the English grand jury might well read: Born in 1166 to increase accusations of crime, lived to be termed the palladium of justice, and died in 1933 of inutility on a wave of economy." Elliff, Notes on the Abolition of the English Grand Jury, 29 JOURNAL OF CRIMINAL LAW and CRIMINOLOGY 3 (1938), quoted in Calkins, Abolition of The Grand Jury Indictment in Illinois, 1966 UNIVERSITY OF ILLINOIS LAW FORUM 423, 428.

[10] Kuckes, the Useful, Dangerous Fiction of Grand Jury Independence, 41 AMERICAN CRIMINAL LAW REVIEW 1 (2004); Simmons, Re-Examining the Grand Jury: Is There Room for Democracy in the Criminal Justice System, 82 BOSTON UNIVERSITY LAW REVIEW 1 (2002); Brenner, Is the Grand Jury Worth Keeping? 81 JUDICATURE 190 (1998); Leipold, Why Grand Juries Do Not (and Cannot) Protect the Accused, 80 CORNELL LAW REVIEW 260 (1995); Poulin, Supervision of the Grand Jury: Who Watches the Guardian?, 68 WASHINGTON UNIVERSITY LAW QUARTERLY 885, 927 (1990); Braun, The Grand Jury — Spirit of the

Community?, 15 ARIZONA LAW REVIEW 893, 915 (1973); Schwartz, Demythologizing the Historic Role of the Grand Jury, 10 AMERICAN CRIMINAL LAW REVIEW 701, 770 (1972); contra, Antell, Modern Grand Jury: Benighted Supergovernment, 51 AMERICAN BAR ASSOCIATION JOURNAL 153, 154; Campbell, Eliminate the Grand Jury, 64 JOURNAL OF CRIMINAL LAW and CRIMINOLOGY 174 (1973).

[11] Brown v. United States, 245 F.2d 549, 554-55 (8th Cir. 1957); United States v. Brown, 49 F.3d 1162, 1168 (6th Cir. 1995); see also, 2 Brenner and Shaw, FEDERAL GRAND JURY: A GUIDE TO LAW AND PRACTICE, §3.2 (2d ed. 2006)(noting that the jurisdiction of the court with which the grand jury is associated includes both territorial and extraterritorial jurisdiction).

[12] United States v. Brown, 49 F.3d at 1168 (6th Cir. 1995); United States v. Williams, 993 F.2d 451, 454-55 (5th Cir. 1993); In re Marc Rich and Co., 707 F.2d 663, 667 (2d Cir. 1983); Blair v. United States, 250 U.S. 273, 283 (1919); United States v. Neff, 212 F.2d 297, 301-302 (3d Cir. 1954).

[13] United States v. Williams, 504 U.S. 36, 48 (1992), quoting, United States v. R. Enterprises, Inc., 498 U.S. 292, 297 (1991) and United States v. Morton Salt Co., 338 U.S. 632, 642-43 (1950); see also, In re Grand Jury, John Doe No. G.J. 2005-2, 478 F.3d 581, 584 (4th Cir. 2007).

[14] Branzburg v. Hayes, 408 U.S. 665, 701 (1972); United States v. York, 428 F.3d 1325, 1332 (11th Cir. 2005).

[15] Blair v. United States, 250 U.S. 273, 282 (1919).

[16] Branzburg v. Hayes, 408 U.S. at 701; see also, United States v. R. Enterprises, Inc., 498 U.S. 292, 297 (1991)(The grand jury may "inquire into all information that might possibly bear on its investigation until it has identified an offense or has satisfied itself that none has occurred"); In re Grand Jury, John Doe No. G.J. 2005-2, 478 F.3d 581, 584 (4th Cir. 2007).

[17] F.R.Crim.P. 6(a).

[18] 18 U.S.C. 3331. The districts eligible by size (those with estimated populations of more than 4 million) appear to include: the District for Arizona; the Central and Northern Districts for California; the District for Colorado, the Middle and Southern Districts for Florida; the Northern District for Georgia; the Northern District for Illinois; the District for Maryland; the District for Massachusetts; the Eastern District for Michigan; the District for Minnesota; the District for

New Jersey; the Eastern and Southern Districts for New York; the Northern and Southern Districts for Ohio; the Eastern and Western Districts for Pennsylvania; the District for South Carolina, the Northern, Southern, and Western Districts for Texas; the Eastern District of Virginia; and the Western District for Washington, 28 U.S.C. 81-131; State and County QuickFacts, available on Jan. 2, 2008 at [http://quickfacts.census.gov./index.html]. Special grand juries are distinctive in that they may serve for longer terms than a regular grand jury and have explicit reporting authority, 18 U.S.C. 3331-3334.

[19] 1 Holdsworth, HISTORY OF ENGLISH LAW, 148 (1903); 2 Hale, HISTORY OF PLEAS OF THE CROWN, 154 (1778 ed.).

[20] Younger, THE PEOPLE'S PANEL: THE GRAND JURY IN THE UNITED STATES, 1634-1941, 5-26 (1963); Goebel and Naughton, LAW ENFORCEMENT IN COLONIAL NEW YORK: A STUDY IN CRIMINAL PROCEDURE (1664-1776), 333-34 n.29 (1970); BOOK OF GENERAL LAWS AND LIBERTYES CONCERNING THE INHABITANTS OF THE MASSACHUSETTS, 47 (1660).

[21] 1 Stat. 88 (1789); 2 Stat. 82 (1800); 5 Stat. 394 (1840); 21 Stat. 43 (1879); 36 Stat. 1164 (1911); 28 U.S.C. 411, 412 (1946 ed.).

[22] 28 U.S.C. 1861-1869.

[23] 28 U.S.C. 1865.

[24] 28 U.S.C. 1862.

[25] 28 U.S.C. 1861.

[26] 28 U.S.C. 1867; F.R.Crim.P. 6(b); Carter v. Jury Commission of Greene County, 396 U.S. 320 (1970); Turner v. Fouche, 396 U.S. 346 (1970); United States v. Raszkiewicz, 169 F.3d 459, 462-63 (7th Cir. 1999); Duren v. Missouri, 439 U.S. 357, 364 (1979); United States v. Artero, 121 F.3d 1256, 1260 (9th Cir. 1997)("To establish a prima facie case for violation of the fair cross section requirement a person challenging the venire must show distinctiveness of the group excluded, unreasonable representation of that group, and that the underrepresentation of that group was caused by systematic exclusion"); United States v. Mitchell, 502 F.3d 931, 950 (9th Cir. 2007); United States v. Gonzalez-Velez, 466 F.3d 27, 39 (1st Cir. 2006); United States v. Henderson, 409 F.3d 1293, 1305 (11th Cir. 2005); see also, Campbell v. Louisiana, 523 U.S. 392 (1998) (white criminal defendant has standing to raise equal protection and due process challenges to state grand jury practices which unconstitutionally excluded members of racial minorities).

[27] "A preliminary draft of Rule 6(b) would have permitted challenge of grand jurors on the grounds of bias and prejudice. This was not included in the final draft, apparently on the view that the grand jury, which merely prefers the charge, should be scrupulously fair but not necessarily uninformed or impartial. Thus cases have held that an attack for bias will not lie." 1 Wright, FEDERAL PRACTICE and PROCEDURE: CRIMINAL 3D, §102 (1999 and 2007 Supp.), citing Estes v. United States, 335 F.2d 609 (5th Cir. 1964); In re Grand Jury, 508 F.Supp. 1210 (S.D.Ala. 1980); United States v. Partin, 320 F.Supp. 275 (E.D. La. 1970); United States v. Knowles, 147 F.Supp. 19 (D.D.C. 1957).

[28] 1 Wright, FEDERAL PRACTICE and PROCEDURE: CRIMINAL 3D, §102 (1999 and 2007 Supp.); see also, United States v. Moore, 811 F.Supp. 112, 117 (W.D.N.Y. 1992); United States v. Finley, 705 F.Supp. 1297, 1306 (N.D. Ill. 1988); United States v. Burke, 700 F.2d 70, 82 (2d Cir. 1983); United States v. Serubo, 604 F.2d 807, 816 (3d Cir. 1979); United States v. York, 428 F.3d 1325, 1332-333 (11th Cir. 2005)(parallel citations omitted)("York has failed to establish that publicity surrounding his case 'substantially influenced' the ultimate decision to indict him and thereby caused him actual prejudice. Bank of Nova Scotia v. United States, 487 U.S. 250, 256 (1988)(dismissal of indictment due to error in grand jury proceedings is only appropriate where 'it is established that the violation substantially influenced the grand jury's decision to indict,' or if there is 'grave doubt' that the decision to indict was free from the substantial influence of such violations'").

[29] In the oath commonly used, grand jurors swear "not to present or indict any persons through hatred, malice nor ill will; nor leave any person unpresented or unindicted through fear, favor, or affection, nor for any reward, or hope or promise thereof. . . ." 1 Beale et al., GRAND JURY LAW AND PRACTICE, §4:4 (1998); see e.g., United States v. Ziesman, 409 F.3d 941, 949 (8th Cir. 2005)("it cannot be assumed that grand jurors will violate their oath to indict no one because of prejudice solely because an individual has lied to them on a matter material to the grand jury's investigation").

[30] 18 U.S.C. 3321; F.R.Crim.P. 6(a).

[31] A grand jury may not be empaneled initially with fewer than 16 members, 18 U.S.C. 3321. This and the statements in section 3321 and Rule 6(a) that federal grand juries shall consist of 16 to 23 members has apparently lead to the conclusion that after a panel is

convened it is in session only if 16 or more of its members are present, 1 Beale et al., GRAND JURY LAW AND PRACTICE, §4:8 (1998); 1 Brenner and Shaw, FEDERAL GRAND JURY: A GUIDE TO LAW AND PRACTICE, §5:17 (2d ed. 2006); United States Department of Justice, FEDERAL GRAND JURY PRACTICE, §2.4 (Aug. 2000); United States v. Leverage Funding Systems, Inc., 637 F.2d 645, 648 (9th Cir. 1980). But for this deeply held view which neither Congress nor Court have sought to change, an argument might made for a quorum of 12, the number required for indictment. Otherwise, it might be argued that dissenting panel members, unable to prevent indictment by their votes, might do so by their absence or departure.

[32] F.R.Crim.P. 6(f).

[33] "The sheriff of every county [was] bound to return to every session of the peace, and every commission of oyer and terminer, and of general gaol delivery, twenty-four good and lawful men of the county, some out of every hundred, to inquire, present, do, and execute all those things, which on the part of our lord the king shall then and there be commanded of them. . . . As many as appear upon this panel are sworn upon the grand jury, to the amount of twelve at least, and not more than twenty-three. . . ." 4 Blackstone, COMMENTARIES 276 (1813 ed.); 1 Hale, HISTORY OF PLEAS OF THE CROWN, 161 (1778 ed.).

[34] The Supreme Court has referred to "Lord Coke's explanation that the number of twelve is much respected in holy writ, as 12 apostles, 12 stones, 12 tribes, etc. . . ." in an effort to explain why the number 12 was chosen for the size of the petit jury, Williams v. Florida, 399 U.S. 78, 81 (1970). Blackstone alludes to the importance of concurrence of twelve grand jurors in the indictment, "for so tender is the law of England of the lives of the subjects, that no man can be convicted at the suit of the king of any capital offense, unless by the unanimous voice of twenty-four of his equals and neighbors: that is, by twelve at least of the grand jury. . . and afterwards, by the whole petit jury, of twelve more," 4 Blackstone, supra at 279. This, in turn he finds to explain the maximum size of the grand jury panel, "As many as appear upon this panel are sworn upon the grand jury, to the amount of twelve at least, but not more than twenty-three; that twelve may be a majority," id. at 276 (emphasis added). Blackstone's view is reflected in some of the earlier cases: "By the act of congress of March 3, 1865 (13 Stat. 500), it is provided that

grand juries in the courts of the United States 'shall consist of not less than sixteen and not exceeding twenty-three persons, . . . and that no indictment shall be found without the concurrence of at least twelve grand jurors.' The earlier authorities show that the accusing body now called the grand jury originally consisted of twelve persons, and all were required to concur. The number was subsequently enlarged to twenty-three, which was the maximum. Undoubtedly one reason why both at common law and by act of congress more jurors are required to be summoned, and by the act of congress to be impaneled than are necessary to find a bill, is to prevent, on the one hand, the course of justice from being defeated if the accused should have one or more friends on the jury; and on the other hand, the better to protect persons against the influence of unfriendly jurors on the panel." United States v. Williams, 28 F.Cas.666, 670 (No. 16,716) (C.C.D.Minn. 1871). "The requiring of twenty-three to be summoned, though we have found no reasons stated in the books, was probably in order to make sure of obtaining a full jury of twelve; possible to be sure of having a few over, so that if the accused should have a friend or two upon the panel, the course of justice might not be defeated; possible to prevent a dissolution of the jury by the death or sickness or absence of one or more of the jurors, or it may be for all these reasons combined." State v. Ostrander, 18 Iowa 435, 443 (1865).

[35] See, 1 Beale et al., GRAND JURY LAW AND PRACTICE, §4:8 n.7 (1998 and 2007-2008 Supp.) for a survey of state provisions, only a half dozen of which reduce the size of grand jury panels below twelve.

[36] One of the few to do so recommended reduction to panels of seven, nine or eleven, with the concurrence of seven required for indictment, Sullivan and Bachman, If It Ain't Broke, Don't Fix It: Why the Grand Jury's Accusatory Function Should Not Be Changed, 75 JOURNAL OF CRIMINAL LAW and CRIMINOLOGY 1047, 1068-69 (1984).

[37] F.R.Crim.P. 6(a)(2).

[38] Hale v. Hensel, 201 U.S. 43, 60 (1906); for a model grand jury oath see, note 28, supra.

[39] F.R.Crim.P. 6(c).

[40] Although there is no requirement that the court charge the jury, it is a practice of long standing, Charge to the Grand Jury, 30 F. Cas. 992 (No. 18255) (C.C.D.Cal. 1872)(Field, J.); 1 Beale et al., GRAND

JURY LAW AND PRACTICE, §4:5 (1998) (model grand jury charge); United States v. Navarro-Vargas, 408 F.3d 1184, 1208 (9th Cir. 2005)(upholding the constitutionality of the model charge).

[41] F.R.Crim.P. 6(g).

[42] 18 U.S.C. 3331, 3333.

[43] "Although the grand jury normally operates, of course, in the courthouse and under judicial auspices, its institutional relationship with the Judicial Branch has traditionally been, so to speak, at arm's length. Judges' direct involvement in the functioning of the grand jury has generally been confined to the constitutive one of calling the grand jurors together and administering their oaths of office." United States v. Williams, 504 U.S. 36, 47 (1992); In re Grand Jury Proceedings (John Roe, Inc.), 142 F.3d 1416, 1425 (11th Cir. 1998); In re Impounded, 241 F.3d 308, 312 (3d Cir. 2001).

[44] At one time, only members of the grand jury could be present when the panel was deliberating or voting, F.R.Crim.P. 6(d)(18 U.S.C.App. (1994 ed.)) the rule has been changed to permit the presence during deliberations and voting of interpreters assigned to assist hearing or speech impaired jurors, F.R.Crim.P. 6(d).

[45] United States v. Zarattini, 552 F.2d 753, 756 (7th Cir. 1977); In re April 1956 Term Grand Jury, 239 F.2d 263, 268-69 (7th Cir. 1957).

[46] United States v. Wiseman, 172 F.3d 1196, 1204-205 (10th Cir. 1999); United States v. Wadlington, 233 F.3d 1067, 1075 (8th Cir. 2000); Lopez v. Department of Justice, 393 F.3d 1345, 1349 (D.C. Cir. 2005).

[47] United States v. Sigma Intern, Inc., 196 F.3d 1314, 1323 (11th Cir. 1999)("A prosecutor's job is to present evidence of criminal activity to a grand jury. In so doing, the prosecutor may explain why a piece of evidence is legally significant. . ."); see generally, 1 Beale et al., GRAND JURY LAW AND PRACTICE §4.15 (1998 and 2007-2008 Supp.).

[48] A subpoena is an order of the court demanding that an individual appear at one of its proceedings and produce evidence on a matter then under consideration. There are two kinds of subpoenas – subpoenas ad testificandum and subpoenas duces tecum. The first is simply a command to appear and testify, the second not only demands the witness's presence at a certain time and place but requires him to bring certain evidence with him. Federal law with regard to subpoenas in criminal cases is governed in large measure by Rule 17 of the Federal Rules of Criminal Procedure: A subpoena

must state the court's name and the title of the proceeding, include the seal of the court, and command the witness to attend and testify at the time and place the subpoena specifies. The clerk must issue a blank subpoena--signed and sealed--to the party requesting it, and that party must fill in the blanks before the subpoena is served. ** *

The court (other than a magistrate judge) may hold in contempt a witness who, without adequate excuse, disobeys a subpoena issued by a federal court in that district. A magistrate judge may hold in contempt a witness who, without adequate excuse, disobeys a subpoena issued by that magistrate judge as provided in 28 U.S.C. § 636(e). F.R.Crim.P. 17(a), (g).

[49] In re Snoonian, 502 F.2d 110, 112 (1st Cir. 1974).

[50] United States v. Calandra, 414 U.S. 338, 343 (1974); cf., United States v. Williams, 504 U.S. 36, 48-9 (1992).

[51] Lopez v. Department of Justice, 393 F.3d 1345, 1349 (D.C. Cir. 2005)("the term 'grand jury subpoena' is in some respects a misnomer, because the grand jury itself does not decide whether to issue the subpoena; the prosecuting attorney does"); Coronado v. Bank Atlantic Bancorp, Inc., 222 F.3d 1315, 1320 (11th Cir. 2000). Subpoenas duces tecum will in fact frequently permit alternative means of compliance under which the witness is given the option of presenting the documents to the attorney for government who is assisting the grand jury, see e.g., the appendices in In re Grand Jury Proceedings (B and J Peanut Co.), 887 F.Supp. 288, 291 (M.D.Ga. 1995), and United States v. International Paper Co., 457 F.Supp. 571, 577 (S.D.Tex. 1978). But see, United States v. Wadlington, 233 F.3d 1067, 1075 (8th Cir. 2000)("The Government rests on its authority to subpoena witnesses in advance of their presentation to the grand jury in order to allow for the efficient presentation of evidence and to save time for grand jurors. See United States v. Universal Mfg. Co., 525 F.2d 808, 811-12 (8th Cir. 1975)(holding that the Government may have advance access to documents and other evidentiary matter subpoenaed by or presented to a federal grand jury); see also In re Possible Violations of 18 U.S.C. §§201, 371, 491 F.Supp. 211, 213 (D.D.C. 1980)(holding that the Government may call a grand jury witness to its offices pursuant to subpoena on the day of grand jury proceedings for a consensual interview so that government attorneys may identify the nature of the proposed testimony). . . . Rule 17(a) of the Federal Rules of Criminal Procedure states that a subpoena 'shall command each person to

whom it is directed to attend and give testimony at the time and place specified therein.' This language has been interpreted to mean that witnesses may be subpoenaed to give testimony at formal proceedings, such as grand jury proceedings, preliminary hearings, and trials. It does not authorize the Government to use grand jury subpoenas to compel prospective grand jury witnesses to attend private interviews with government agents"); Lopez v. Department of Justice, 393 F.3d at 1349 ("the prosecutor may issue the subpoena without the knowledge of the grand jury, but his authority to do so is grounded in the grand jury investigation, not the prosecutor's own inquiry. Federal prosecutors have no authority to issue grand jury subpoenas independent of the grand jury").

[52] "Whenever a witness in any proceeding before. . . any. . . grand jury of the United States refuses without just cause shown to comply with an order of the court to testify or provide other information. . . the court. . . may summarily order his confinement at a suitable place until such time as the witness is willing to given such testimony or provide such information. . . ." 28 U.S.C. 1826(a). "[C]ivil contempt . . . is remedial, and for the benefit of the complainant. [C]riminal contempt . . . is punitive to vindicate the authority of the court. . . . [T]he relief . . .is remedial if the defendant stands committed unless and until he performs the affirmative act required by the court's order. . . ." Hicks v. Feiock, 485 U.S. 624, 631-32 (1988). Civil contempt is imposed "for the obvious purpose of compelling the witnesses to obey the orders to testify. . . . However, the justification for coercive imprisonment as applied to civil contempt depends upon the ability of the contemnor to comply with the court's order. Where the grand jury has been finally discharged a contumacious witness can no longer be confined since he then has no further opportunity to purge himself of contempt." Shillitani v. United States, 384 U.S. 364, 368, 371 (1966). In the case of civil contempt under section 1826, the recalcitrant witness must be released after eighteen months even if the grand jury has not been discharged, In re Grand Jury Proceedings of the Special April 2002 Grand Jury, 347 F.3d 197, 206 (7th Cir. 2003). While fear is no just cause for failure to obey a grand jury subpoena, the witness's fear is a factor to be considered in determining whether civil contempt is likely to induce compliance. In re Grand Jury Proceeding (Doe), 13 F.3d 459, 461 (1st Cir. 1994); In re Grand Jury Proceedings, 914 F.2d 1372, 1374-375 (9th Cir. 1990); In re Grand Jury Proceedings of Dec., 1989, 903 F.2d 1167,

1169 (7th Cir. 1990); In re Grand Jury Proceedings, 862 F.2d 430, 432 (2d Cir. 1988).

[53] "A court of the United States shall have power to punish by fine or imprisonment, at its discretion, such contempt of its authority, and none other, as . . . (3) Disobedience or resistance to its lawful writ, process, order, rule, decree, or command," 18 U.S.C. 401.

[54] United States v. Marquardo, 149 F.3d 36, 39-41 (1st Cir. 1998); In re Grand Jury Proceedings (Goodman), 33 F.3d 1060, 1061 (9th Cir. 1994); In re Grand Jury Witness, 835 F.2d 437, 440 (2d Cir. 1987); United States v. Ryan, 810 F.2d 650, 653 (7th Cir. 1987); United States v. Alvarez, 489 F.Supp.2d 714, 719-20 (W.D. Tex. 2007).

[55] "Whoever. . . having taken an oath before a competent tribunal, officer, or person, in any case in which a law of the United States authorizes an oath to be administered, that he will testify. . . truly, . . . willfully and contrary to such oath states. . . any material matter which he does not believe to be true . . . is guilty of perjury and shall . . . be fined under this title or imprisoned not more than five years, or both. . . ." 18 U.S.C. 1621.

[56] "(a) Whoever under oath. . . in any proceeding before. . . any . . . grand jury of the United States knowingly makes any false material declaration. . . shall be fined under this title or imprisoned not more than five years, or both. . . . "(c). . . . In any prosecution under this section, the falsity of a declaration . . . shall be established sufficient for conviction by proof that the defendant while under oath made irreconcilably contradictory declarations material to the point in question in any proceeding before. . . any . . . grand jury. It shall be a defense . . . . that the defendant at the time he made each declaration believed the declaration was true. "(d) Where, in the same continuous . . . grand jury proceeding in which a declaration is made, the person making the declaration admits such declaration to be false, such admission shall bar prosecution under this section if, at the time the admission is made, the declaration has not substantially affected the proceeding, or it has not become manifest hat such falsity has been or will be exposed. . . ." 18 U.S.C. 1623.

[57] In re Application of Wood, 833 F.2d 113, 116 (8th Cir. 1987); In re New Haven Grand Jury, 604 F.Supp. 453, 455-56 (D.Conn. 1985). Section 1504 of title 18 of the United States Code provides, "Whoever attempts to influence the action or decision of any grand. . . juror of any court of the United States upon any issue or matter pending before such juror, or before the jury of which he is a

member, or pertaining to his duties, by writing or sending to him any written communication, in relation to issue or matter, shall be fined under this title or imprisoned not more than six months, or both. Nothing in this section shall be construed to prohibit the communication of a request to appear before the grand jury."

[58] United States v. Williams, 504 U.S. 36, 52 (1992); United States v. Mandujano, 425 U.S. 564, 581 (1976); United States v. Fritz, 852 F.2d 1175, 1178 (9th Cir. 1988); United States v. Pabian, 704 F.2d 1533, 1538-539 (11th Cir.1983); United States v. Arena, 894 F. Supp. 580, 585 (N.D.N.Y. 1995); but see, In re Application of Wood, 833 F.2d 113, 116 (8th Cir. 1987)(court may permit a matter to be presented to the grand jury by a private individual, if the prosecutor declines to do so; the decision to prosecute, however, rests with the attorney for the government, should the grand jury vote to indict). It has been suggested that targets be afforded the opportunity to appear before the grand jury as a matter of right, Arnella, Reforming the Federal Grand Jury and the State Preliminary Hearing to Prevent Conviction Without Adjudication, 78 MICHIGAN LAW REVIEW 463, 569 (1980).

[59] United States v. Williams, 504 U.S. 36, 51-4 (1992); United States v. Mahalick, 498 F.3d 475, 479-80 (7th Cir. 2007).

[60] Blair v. United States, 250 U.S. 273, 280-81 (1919); Barry v. United States ex rel. Cunningham, 279 U.S. 597, 617 (1929); Stein v. New York, 346 U.S. 156, 184 (1953).

[61] 18 U.S.C. 3144, 3142. The procedure applies to witnesses "in a criminal proceeding," a class which includes material grand jury witnesses, United States v. Awadallah, 349 F.3d 42, 49-51 (2d Cir. 2003); Bacon v. United States, 449 F.2d 933, 936-41 (9th Cir. 1971). See generally, Arrest and Detention of Material Witnesses: Federal Law in Brief and Section 12 of the USA PATRIOT and Terrorism Prevention Reauthorization Act (H.R.3199), CRS REP. RL33077 (Sept. 8, 2005); Boyle, The Material Witness Statute Post September 11: Why It Should Not Include Grand Jury Witnesses, 48 NEW YORK LAW SCHOOL LAW REVIEW 12 (2003).

[62] United States v. Mandujano, 425 U.S. 564, 572 (1976).

[63] E.g., In re Sealed Case (Lewinsky), 162 F.3d 670, 674 n.4 (D.C. Cir. 1998)("[Exception as noted below,] [n]o grand jury witness may refuse to answer questions on the ground that the questions are based on illegally obtained evidence").

[64] United States v. Calandra, 414 U.S. 338, 345 (1974)("In Branzburg v. Hayes, [408 U.S. 665,] 682 and 688, the Court noted '[c]itizens generally are not constitutionally immune from grand jury subpoenas . . .' and that 'the longstanding principle that the public . . . has a right to every man's evidence . . . is particularly applicable to grand jury proceedings.' The duty to testify may on occasion be burdensome and even embarrassing. It may cause injury to a witness' social and economic status. Yet the duty to testify has been regarded as 'so necessary to the administration of justice' that the witness' personal interest in privacy must yield to the public's overriding interest in full disclosure"); Grand Jury Proceedings (Williams) v. United States, 995 F.2d 1013, 1016 (11th Cir. 1993).

[65] The question of whether a protective order arising out of federal civil litigation takes precedence over a grand jury subpoena for material covered by the order has divided the federal courts of appeal. One approach requires the demonstration of a compelling need or of extraordinary circumstances before the secrecy of a protective order can be breached, while others take the position that grand jury subpoenas trump protective orders. In re Grand Jury Subpoena (Roach), 138 F.3d 442 (1st Cir. 1998) describes the split among the circuits over precisely when a pre-existing protective order should take precedence over a grand jury subpoena. The Fourth, Ninth, and Eleventh Circuits have adopted a per se rule under which "the existence of an otherwise valid protective order [is] not sufficient grounds to quash the subpoena duces tecum issued by the grand jury," 138 F.3d at 444, citing In re Grand Jury Subpoena, 836 F.2d 1468, 1478 (4th Cir. 1988); In re Grand Jury Subpoena, 62 F.3d 1222, 1224 (9th Cir. 1995); and In re Grand Jury Proceedings, 995 F.2d 1013, 1020 (11th Cir. 1993). The Second Circuit has espoused a balancing test thought to prefer the protective order over the grand jury subpoena, 138 F.3d at 444-45, citing Martindell v. International Tel. and Tel. Corp., 594 F.2d 291, 295 (2d Cir. 1979); see also, In re Grand Jury Subpoena Dated April 19, 1991, 945 F.2d 1221, 1223-224 (2d Cir. 1991). The First Circuit has endorsed a modified per se rule under which "[a] grand jury's subpoena trumps a Rule 26(c) protective order unless the person seeking to avoid the subpoena can demonstrate the existence of exceptional circumstances that clearly favor subordinating the subpoena to the protective order," 138 F.3d at 445. The Third Circuit agrees with the First, In re Grand Jury, 286 F.3d 153, 157-58 (3d Cir. 2002). See generally, Return to Certainty:

Why Grand Jury Subpoenas Should Supersede Civil Protective Orders, 10 SUFFOLK JOURNAL OF TRIAL AND APPELLATE ADVOCACY 43 (2005).

[66] United States v. Calandra, 414 U.S. at 346; United Stats v. Nixon, 418 U.S. 683, 709 (1974); In re Grand Jury Subpoenas 04-124-03 and 04-124-05, 454 F.3d 511, 520 (6th Cir. 2006); In re Grand Jury, 475 F.3d 1299, 1304 (D.C. Cir. 2007).

[67] F.R.Evid. 1101(c), (d)(2), 501; In re Grand Jury Investigation, 399 F.3d 527, 530 (2d Cir. 2005); In re Impounded, 241 F.3d 308, 313 (3d Cir. 2001).

[68] F.R.Evid. 501. ("Except as otherwise required by the Constitution of the United States or provided by Act of Congress or in rule prescribed by the Supreme Court pursuant to statutory authority, the privilege of a witness, person, government, State, or political subdivision thereof shall be governed by the principles of the common law as they may be interpreted by the courts of the United States in the light of reason and experience. However, in civil actions and proceedings, with respect to an element of a claim or defense as to which State law supplies the rule of decision, the privilege of a witness, person, government, State, or political subdivision thereof shall be determined in accordance with State law").

[69] Merrill v. Waffle House, Inc., 227 F.R.D. 467, 471 (N.D.Tex. 2005), quoting, Whalen v. Roe, 429 U.S. 589, 602 n.28 (1977)("physician-patient privilege is unknown to the common law"); United States v. Bek, 493 F.3d 790, 801-802 (7th Cir. 2007); Northwestern Memorial Hospital v. Ashcroft, 362 F.3d 923, 927 (7th Cir. 2004); Galarza v. United States, 179 F.R.D. 291, 294 (S.D.Cal. 1998); Gilbreath v. Guadalupe Hospital Foundation Inc., 5 F.3d 785, 791 (5th Cir. 1993).

[70] United States v. Arthur Young and Co., 465 U.S. 805, 817 (1984); United States v. Bisanti, 414 F.3d 168, 170 (1st Cir. 2005); In re Grand Jury Proceedings(Tullen), 220 F.3D 568, 571 (7th Cir. 2000); Inspector General v. Glenn, 122 F.3d 1007, 1012 (11th Cir. 1997).

[71] In re Grand Jury Proceedings (Scarce), 5 F.3d 397, 403 (9th Cir. 1993); United States v. Doe, 460 F.2d 328, 333-34 (1st Cir. 1972); but see, Cusumano v. Microsoft Corp., 162 F.3d 708, 714-15 (1st Cir. 1998)(recognizing qualified journalist-like privilege).

[72] United States v. Dunford, 148 F.3d 385, 390-91 (4th Cir. 1998); In re Grand Jury, 103 F.3d 1140. 1146 (3d Cir. 1997); United States v. Duran, 884 F.Supp. 537, 541 (D.D.C. 1995); contra, In re Grand

Jury Proceedings, Unemancipated Minor Child, 949 F.Supp. 1487, 1497 (E.D.Wash. 1996).

[73] United States v. Schoenheinz,548 F.2d 1389, 1390 (9th Cir. 1977).

[74] American Elec. Power Co., 191 F.R.D. 132, 141 (S.D.Ohio 1999); Delozier v. First National Bank, 109 F.R.D. 161, 163-64 (E.D.Tenn. 1986); Harris v. United States, 413 F.2d 316, 319-20 (9th Cir. 1969).

[75] In re Verplank, 329 F.Supp. 433, 436-37 (S.D.N.Y. 1970).

[76] United States v. Foster, 986 F.2d 541, 542-44 (D.C.Cir. 1993).

[77] United States v. Simmons, 964 F.2d 763, 768-79 (8th Cir. 1992).

[78] Linde Thompson Langworthy Kohn and Van Dyke v. RTC, 5 F.3d 1508, 1514 (D.C.Cir. 1993); Petersen v. Douglas County Bank and Trust Co., 967 F.2d 1186, 1188 (8th Cir. 1992).

[79] University of Pennsylvania v. EEOC, 493 U.S. 182, 188-95 (1990); Leon v. County of San Diego, 202 F.R.D. 631, 637 (S.D.Cal. 2001).

[80] Virmani v. Novant Health Inc., 259 F.3d 284, 286-93 (4th Cir. 2001); Mattice v. Memorial Hospital, 203 F.R.D. 381, 384-86 (N.D.Ind. 2001)(collecting cases); Braswell v. Haywood Regional Medical Center, 352 F.Supp.2d 639, 651 (W.D.N.C. 2005); Agster v. Maricopa County, 422 F.3d 836, 839 (9th Cir. 2005); Adkins v. Christie, 488 F.3d 1324, 1330 (11th Cir. 2007).

[81] Pearson v. Miller, 211 F.3d 57, 69 (3d Cir. 2000).

[82] In re Grand Jury Subpoena Dated Dec. 17, 1996, 148 F.3d 487, 492-93 (5th Cir. 1998); other than in cases of grand jury subpoenas, two lower federal courts have recognized a qualified mediation privilege, Sheldone v. Pennsylvania Turnpike Comm., 104 F.Supp.2d 511, 512-18 (W.D.Pa. 2000); Folb v. Motion Picture Industry Pension and Health Plans, 16 F.Supp.2d 1164, 1170-181 (C.D.Cal. 1998).

[83] In re Grand Jury Subpoenas Dated Jan. 20, 1998, 995 F.Supp. 332, 334-37 (E.D.N.Y. 1998).

[84] In re Sealed Case (Secret Service), 148 F.3d 1073, 1079 (D.C.Cir. 1998).

[85] In re Subpoena Issued to Commodity Futures Trading Commission, 370 F.Supp.2d 201, 209-12 (D.D.C. 2005)(rejecting privilege but citing division among the lower federal courts); contra, Goodyear Tire and Rubber Co. v. Chiles Power Supply, Inc., 332 F.3d 976, 979-82 (6th Cir. 2003).

[86] United States Department of Education v. National Collegiate Athletic Association, 481 F.3d 936, 938 (7th Cir. 2007).

[87] Branzburg v. Hayes, 408 U.S. 665 (1972); In re Grand Jury Proceedings (Scarce), 5 F.3d 397, 403 (9th Cir. 1993); Storer Communications, Inc. v. Giovan, 810 F.2d 580, 584-85 (6th Cir. 1987); see also, In re Grand Jury Subpoena, Judith Miller, 397 F.3d 964, 968-73 (D.C.Cir. 2005)(holding that no First Amendment privilege existed in a grand jury context, but noting disagreement within the panel over whether a qualified common law journalist privilege (unavailable under the facts before court) might exist), but see, New York Times v. Gonzales, 382 F.Supp.2d 457, 493 (S.D.N.Y. 2005)(recognizing common law privilege in a grand jury context).

[88] Freiermuth v. PPG Industries, Inc., 218 F.R.D. 694, 697 (N.D.Ala. 2003)(citing the circuits that have refused to recognize the privilege); In re Kaiser Aluminum and Chemical Co., 214 F.3d 586, 593 (5th Cir. 2000) (declining to recognize privilege when asserted against the government); Bredice v. Doctor's Hospital, Inc., 50 F.R.D. 249, 251 (D.D.C.1970), aff'd, 479 F.2d 920 (D.C.Cir. 1973)(privilege recognized); Reichhold Chemicals, Inc. v. Textron, Inc., 157 F.R.D. 522, 524-25 (N.D.Fla. 1994); In re Grand Jury Proceedings (File Sealed), 861 F.Supp. 386, 389-91 (D.Md. 1994)(privilege not applicable to grand jury matters).

[89] In re Sealed Case (Espy), 121 F.3d 729, 742-57 (D.C.Cir. 1997)(recognizing qualified privilege may be available to quash grand jury subpoena); In re Lindsay, 158 F.3d 1263, 1266 (D.C.Cir. 1998); Cheney v. United States District Court, 542 U.S. 367, 382-90(2004).

[90] Orange v. City of Suffolk, 855 F.Supp. 620, 622-24 (E.D.N.Y. 1994).

[91] Cf., Pierce County v. Guillen, 537 U.S. 129, 143-45 (2003)(scope of federal statutory privilege protecting official documents compiled to identify hazardous highway conditions).

[92] United States v. Reynolds, 345 U.S.1, 6-7 (1953)(recognizing privilege); Al-Haramain Islamic Foundation v. Bush, 507 F.3d 1190, 1196 (D.C. Cir. 2007); El-Masri v. United States, 479 F.3d 296, 303 (4th Cir. 2007); Crater Corp. v. Lucent Technologies, Inc., 255 F.3d 1361, 1370 (Fed.Cir. 2001); In re Sealed Case (Epsy), 121 F.3d at 736; Bareford v. General Dynamics Corp., 973 F.2d 1138, 1141 (5th Cir. 1993); cf., Tenet v. Doe, 544 U. S. 1, 9 (2005)(holding that the "well-established" state secrets privilege has not replaced the Totten rule).

[93] Schneiber v. Society for Savings Bancorp, Inc., 11 F.3d 217, 220 (D.C.Cir. 1993) (recognizing privilege); Principle v. Crossland Savings, FSB, 149 F.R.D. 444, 447 (E.D.N.Y. 1993).

[94] In re Production of Records to Grand Jury, 618 F.Supp. 440 (D.Mass. 1985)(social worker communications); In re Grand Jury Subpoena, 144 F.Supp.2d 540, 541-42 (W.D.Va. 2001)(state tax records).

[95] Dept. of Interior v. Klamath Water Users, 532 U.S. 1, 7-9 (2001); Judicial Watch, Inc. v. Food and Drug Administration, 449 F.3d 141, (D.C. Cir. 2006); United States v. Zingsheim, 384 F.3d 867, 872 (7th Cir. 2004); Tigue v. U.S. Department of Justice, 312 F.3d 70, 76 (2d Cir. 2002); United States v. Fernandez, 231 F.3d 1240, 1246-247 (9th Cir. 2000); Texaco Puerto Rico v. Department of Consumer Affairs, 60 F.3d 867, 884-85 (1st Cir.1995).

[96] Kientzy v. McDonnell Douglas Corp., 133 F.R.D. 570, 571 (E.D.Mo. 1991)(recognizing privilege).

[97] In re Green Grand Jury, 492 F.3d 976, 979 (8th Cir. 2007); In re Grand Jury Subpoena, 419 F.3d 329, 338-39 (5th Cir. 2005); In re Grand Jury Subpoena Under Seal, 415 F.3d 333, 338 (4th Cir. 2005); In re Grand Jury Subpoena (Newparent, Inc.), 274 F.3d 563, 571 (1st Cir. 2001); In re Subpoenaed Grand Jury Witness, 171 F.3d 511, 513 (7th Cir. 1999); Ralls v. United States, 52 F.3d 223, 225-27 (9th Cir. 1995);cf., Swidler and Berlin v. United States, 524 U.S. 399, 410-11 (1998) (holding that the attorney-client privilege survives the death of the client where the privilege had been asserted in the face of a grand jury subpoena).

[98] In re Green Grand Jury, 492 F.3d 976, 979 (8th Cir. 2007); In re Grand Jury Subpoena, 419 F.3d 329, 339 (5th Cir. 2005); In re Grand Jury Subpoena Dated March 19, 2002 and August 2, 2002, 318 F.3d 379, 383-86 (2d Cir. 2003); United Kingdom v. United States, 238 F.3d 1312, 1321 (11th Cir. 2001); cf., In re Grand Jury Proceedings (John Doe Co.), 350 F.3d 299, 301-4(2d Cir. 2003)(holding the work product privilege had not been waived or forfeited).

[99] In re Grand Jury Investigation, 918 F.2d 374, 384-85 (3d Cir. 1990).

[100] In re Grand Jury Investigation (Detroit Police Department Special Cash Fund), 922 F.2d 1266, 1270-272 (6th Cir. 1991); Does I thru XXII v. Advanced Textile Corp., 214 F.3d 1058, 1072 (9th Cir. 2000); Commonwealth of Puerto Rico v. United States, 490 F.3d 50, 62-4 (1st Cir. 2007)(recognizing a more broadly stated law

enforcement privilege); In re United States Department of Homeland Security, 459 F.3d 565, 569-70 (5th Cir. 2006)(same).

[101] Trammel v. United States, 445 U.S. 40, 53 (1980); United States v. Thompson, 454 F.3d 459, 464 (5th Cir. 2006); United States v. Vo, 413 F.3d 1010, 1016 (9th Cir. 2005); United States v. Jarvison, 409 F.3d 1221, 1231 (10th Cir. 2005); United States v. Bad Wound, 203 F.3d 1072, 1075 (8th Cir. 2000); United States v. Yerardi, 192 F.3d 14, 17-8 (1st Cir. 1999); United States v. Morris, 988 F.2d 1335, 1338-341 (4th Cir. 1993).

[102] Blau v. United States, 340 U.S. 332 (1951); United States v. Darif, 446 F.3d 701, 705 (7th Cir. 2006); United States v. Griffin, 440 F.3d 1138, 1143-144 (9th Cir. 2006); United States v. Jarvison, 409 F.3d 1221, 1231 (10th Cir. 2005); United States v. Bey, 188 F.3d 1, 4-5 (1st Cir. 1999).

[103] Jaffee v. Redmond, 518 U.S. 1 (1996)(recognizing a generally applicable federal privilege in another context and leaving development of the dimensions of the privilege for another day); United States v. Chase, 340 F.3d 978, 985 (9th Cir. 2003) (refusing to recognize a dangerous patient exception to the federal privilege and noting a circuit split on the issue); In re Grand Jury Investigation (Doe), 114 F.Supp.2d 1054, 1055 (D.Ore. 2000)(holding that a grand jury target had waived his psychotherapist-patient privilege).

[104] Fisher v. United States, 425 U.S. 391, 403 (1976); In re Grand Jury Proceedings #5, 401 F.3d 247, 250 (4th Cir. 2005); In re Grand Jury Subpoena (Newparent, Inc.), 274 F.3d 563, 571 (1st Cir. 2001); In re Grand Jury, 475 F.3d 1299, 1304 (D.C. Cir. 2007).

[105] In re Grand Jury Investigation, No. 06-1474, 445 F.3d 266, 274 (3d Cir. 2006)("The government must make a prima facie showing that (1) the client was committing or intending to commit a fraud or crime, and (2) the attorney-client communications were in furtherance of that alleged crime or fraud "); see also, In re Green Grand Jury Proceedings, 492 F.3d 976, 979 (8th Cir. 2007); In re Grand Jury Subpoena, 419 F.3d 329, 335 (5th Cir. 2005); In re Grand Jury Proceedings, 417 F.3d 18, 22 (1st Cir. 2005); In re Grand Jury Subpoena (No. 00-1622), 223 F.3d 213, 217-19 (3d Cir. 2000); In re Grand Jury Subpoenas(Jane Roe and John Doe), 144 F.3d 653, 659-62 (10th Cir. 1998); cf., United States v. Zolin, 491 U.S. 554, 562-63 (1989).

[106] Gerald B.Lefcourt, P.C. v. United States, 125 F.3d 79, 86-88(2d Cir. 1997); United States v. Ellis, 90 F.3d 447, 450-51 (11th Cir. 1996).

[107] Ralls v. United States, 52 F.3d 223, 225-26 (9th Cir. 1995); In re Grand Jury Proceedings No.92-4, 42 F.3d 876, 878-79 (4th Cir. 1994); Vingelli v. United States (DEA), 992 F.2d 449, 451-54 (2d Cir. 1993). The motion to quash is no more likely to be granted because the prosecutor failed to comply with the guidelines of the United States Attorneys' Manual concerning the issuance of grand jury subpoenas seeking client information, In re Grand Jury Proceedings No. 92-4, 42 F.3d 887, 880 (4th Cir. 1994).

[108] In re Grand Jury Subpoenas (Anderson), 906 F.2d 1485, 1488, 1489, 1492 (10th Cir. 1990); In re Grand Jury Proceedings (Goodman), 33 F.3d 1060, 1063-64 (9th Cir. 1994); Ralls v. United States, 52 F.3d 223, 225-26 (9th Cir. 1995); In re Subpoenaed Grand Jury Witness, 171 F.3d 511, 514 (7th Cir. 1999).

[109] In re Grand Jury Subpoena Dated July 6, 2005, F.3d , (2d Cir. Nov. 16, 2007); In re Sealed Case, 29 F.3d 715, 718 (D.C.Cir. 1994); In re Sealed Case, No. 98-3032, 146 F.3d 881, 884-87 (D.C.Cir. 1998); In re Subpoenaed Grand Jury Witness ("Tom Hagen"), 171 F.3d 511, 514 (7th Cir. 1999); In re Grand Jury Subpoena (Newparent, Inc), 274 F.3d 563, 574 (1st Cir. 2001); In re Grand Jury Subpoena Dated March 19, 2002 and August 2, 2002, 318 F.3d 379, 382-84(2d Cir. 2003); In re Grand Jury Proceedings #5, 401 F.3d 247, 250 (4th Cir. 2005).

[110] In re Green Grand Jury Proceedings, 492 F.3d 976, 979-80 (8th Cir. 2007); In re Grand Jury Subpoena, 419 F.3d 329, 335 (5th Cir. 2005); In re Grand Jury Proceedings #5, 401 F.3d 247, 251 (4th Cir. 2005); In re Sealed Case (RNC), 223 F.3d 775, 778-79 (D.C.Cir. 2000); In re Richard Roe, Inc., 168 F.3d 69, 70-72 (2d Cir. 1999).

[111] In re Grand Jury Subpoena (No. 99-41150 et al.), 220 F.3d 406, 408 (5th Cir. 2000); In re Grand Jury, 419 F.3d 329, 333 n.3 (5th Cir. 2005); In re Grand Jury Proceedings (Rogers and Wells), 43 F.3d 966, 972 (5th Cir. 1994); In re Grand Jury Proceedings Thursday Special Grand Jury, 33 F.3d 342, 349 (4th Cir. 1994).

[112] "In all criminal prosecutions, the accused shall enjoy the right . . . to have the Assistance of Counsel for his defence." U.S.Const. Amend.VI.

[113] "[U]ntil such time as the 'government has committed itself to prosecute, and . . . the adverse positions of the government and defendant have solidified' the Sixth Amendment right to counsel does not attach.' Moran v. Burbine, 475 U.S. 412, 432 (1986), quoting United States v. Gouveia , 467 U.S. 180, 189 (1984) and

Kirby v. Illinois, 406 U.S. 682, 689 (1972); United States v. Hayes, 231 F.3d 663, 675 (9th Cir. 2000); In re Grand Jury Investigation (Kiernan), 182 F.3d 668, 671 (9th Cir. 1999); United States v. Waldon, 363 F.3d 1103, 1112 n.3 (11th Cir. 2004). The right may well apply with regard to questioning of a witness before the grand jury concerning the facts of the witness' prior conviction then pending on appeal, United States v. Kennedy, 372 F.3d 686, 692-93 (4th Cir. 2004).

[114] "The preindictment investigation of Kravit could violate the Sixth Amendment therefore, only if it affected his representation of Van Engel at the later stages of the case, in particular the trial." United States v. Van Engel, 15 F.3d 623, 630 (7th Cir. 1993). "The district court's exercise of its discretion to quash the subpoena because it created a serious interference with Reyes-Requena's relationship with his attorney is justified for several reasons. Reyes-Requena's Sixth Amendment rights had attached. The prosecution against him was moving swiftly – an indictment issued within three weeks of Reyes-Requena's detention hearing. DeGeurin's representation of Reyes-Requena was effectively stalled during the two-to-three week interval that he contested the subpoena. The government made no effort to explain, even rhetorically, why it was necessary to subpoena DeGeurin during that critical juncture in his representation of the defendant. The government made not a single argument in the district court or before this court to suggest that a brief delay in the process, until a lull in the Reyes-Requena prosecution or until after his conviction would have been imprudent." In re Grand Jury Subpoena for Reyes-Requena, 913 F.2d 1118, 1128 (5th Cir. 1990).

[115] United States v. Bergeson, 425 F.3d 1221, 1224-227 (9th Cir. 2005); In re Grand Jury Proceedings (Goodman), 33 F.3d 1060, 1062-63 (9th Cir. 1994); In re Grand Jury Matter (Special Grand Jury Narcotics), 926 F.2d 348, 351 (4th Cir. 1991).

[116] Conn v. Gabbert, 526 U.S. 286, 292 (1999); United States v. Mandujano, 425 U.S. 564, 581 (1976); United States v. McKenna, 327 F.3d 830, 838 (9th Cir. 2003). Although the lower federal courts have generally recognized the right of a grand jury witness to suspend his or her testimony in order to consult with an attorney immediately outside the grand jury room, In re Grand Jury Subpoena (McDougal), 97 F.3d 1090, 1092-93 (8th Cir. 1996); Gabbert v. Conn, 131 F.3d 793, 801 (9th Cir. 1997), rev'd on other grounds, 526 U.S. 526 (1999), as the Supreme Court observed in Conn the Court

itself has never held that such an accommodation is constitutionally required, Conn v. Gabbert, 526 U.S. at 292; In re Grand Jury Investigation (Kiernan), 182 F.3d 668, 671 n.3 (9th Cir. 1999). Subject to various limitations, a number of states permit state grand jury witnesses to have an attorney present when they testify: Ariz. R.Crim.P. 12.6, Ariz.Rev.Stat.Ann. §21-412 (only targets of investigation); Colo.Rev.Stat.Ann. §16-5-204(4)(d); Conn.Gen.Stat. Ann. §54-47f; Fla.Stat.Ann. §905.17; Ill.Comp.Laws Ann. ch.725, §5/112-4.1; Ind.Code Ann. §35-34-2-5.5; Kan.Stat.Ann. §22-3009; La.Code Crim.P.Ann. art.433 (only targets of an investigation); Mass. Gen.Laws Ann. ch.277 §14A; Mich.R.Crim.P. 6.005(I), Mich. Comp.Laws Ann. §767.3; Minn.R.Crim.P. 18.04 (only witnesses who have waived or been granted immunity); Neb.Rev.Stat. §29-1411; Nev.Rev.Stat. §172.239; N.M.Stat. §31-6-4; N.Y.Crim.P.Law §190.52 (only witnesses who have waived immunity); Okla.Stat.Ann. tit.22 §340; Pa.Stat.Ann. tit.42 §4549; S.D.Cod.Laws Ann. §23A-5-11; Utah Code Ann. §77-10a-13; Va.Code Ann. §19.2-209; Wash.Rev.Code Ann. §10.27.120 (unless the witness has been granted immunity); Wis.Stat.Ann. §968.45.

[117] "Congress shall make no law respecting an establishment of religion, or prohibiting the free exercise thereof; or abridging the freedom of speech, or of the press; or the right of the people peaceably to assemble, and to petition the Government for a redress of grievances." U.S.Const. Amend.I.

[118] "[N]ews gathering is not without its First Amendment protections, and grand jury investigations if instituted or conducted other than in good faith, would pose wholly different issues for resolution under the First amendment. Official harassment of the press undertaken not for purposes of law enforcement but to disrupt a reporters' relationship with his news sources would have no justification. Grand juries are subject to judicial control and subpoenas to motions to quash. We do not expect courts will forget that grand juries must operate within the limits of the First Amendment. . . ." Branzburg v. Hayes, 408 U.S. 665, 707-8 (1972).

[119] Branzburg v. Hayes, 408 U.S. 665 (1972)(freedom of the press); Cohen v. Cowles Media Co., 501 U.S. 663, 669 (1991)("the First Amendment does not relieve a newspaper reporter of the obligation shared by all citizens to respond to a grand jury subpoena and answer questions relevant to a grand jury subpoena, even thought the reporter might be required to reveal a confidential source"); In re

Grand Jury Subpoena, Judith Miller, 438 F.3d 1141, 1145-150 (D.C.Cir. 2006)(declining to recognize either a First Amendment or common law privilege under the facts before it); In re Grand Jury Subpoena American Broadcasting Companies, Inc., 947 F.Supp. 1314, 1318-321 (E.D.Ark. 1996); In re Grand Jury 87-3 Subpoena Duces Tecum, 955 F.2d 229, 231-34 (4th Cir. 1992)(freedom of expression); National Commodity and Barter Ass'n v. United States, 951 F.2d 1172, 1174-175 (10th Cir. 1991)("when a party makes a prima facie showing of First Amendment infringement, the government must show a compelling need to obtain the documents identifying petitioner's members. Further, the government must show that the records sought bear a substantial relationship to this compelling interests . . . . A good-faith criminal investigation into possible evasion of reporting requirements through the use of a private banking system that keeps no records is a compelling interest"); In re the Grand Jury Empaneling of the Special Grand Jury, 171 F.3d 826, 835 (3d Cir. 1999)(freedom of religion). The Department of Justice has issued guidelines relating to subpoenas issued to media and its representatives, 28 U.S.C. §50.10, but they do create enforceable legal rights, In re Grand Jury Subpoena, Judith Miller, 438 F.3d 1141, 1152-153 (D.C. Cir. 2006). Reporters, academics and others have periodically suggested adjustments in the law in this area, e.g., Papandrea, Citizen Journalism and the Reporter's Privilege, 91 MINNESOTA LAW REVIEW 515 (2007); Langley and Levine, Branzburg Revisited: Confidential Sources and First Amendment Values, 57 GEORGE WASHINGTON LAW REVIEW 13 (1988); Rood and Grossman, The Case for a Federal Journalist's Testimonial Shield Statute, 18 HASTINGS CONSTITUTIONAL LAW QUARTERLY 779 (1981), an effort which may not be without its own pitfalls, see, Are Oliver Stone and Tom Clancy Journalists: Determining Who Has Standing to Claim the Journalist's Privilege, 69 WASHINGTON LAW REVIEW 739 (1994); Using the Shield as a Sword: an Analysis of How the Current Congressional Proposals for a Reporter's Shield Law Wound the Fifth Amendment, 20 ST. JOHN'S JOURNAL OF LEGAL COMMENTARY 339 (2006).

[120] "The right of the people to be secure in their persons, houses, papers, and effects, against unreasonable searches and seizures, shall not be violated, and no Warrants shall issue, but upon probable cause, supported by Oath or affirmation, and particularly describing the

place to be searched, and the persons or things to be seized." U.S.Const. Amend. IV.

[121] Zurcher v. Stanford Daily, 436 U.S. 547, 575-76 (Stewart, J. dissenting). Of course, the government may respond to a motion to quash by seeking and executing a search warrant for the same material, if it can convince a magistrate that it has probable cause, United States v. Comprehensive Drug Testing, Inc.,473 F.3d 915, 929-31 (9th Cir. 2006).

[122] Forthwith subpoenas command the witness to appear immediately, thereby reducing the possibility of filing a timely motion to quash or to seek the assistance of counsel, and raising questions as to when a forthwith subpoena is really an arrest or search warrant available without the necessities of the Fourth Amendment.

[123] United States v. Suskind, 4 F.3d 1400, 1401 (6th Cir. 1993), adopting Part IV of its previously vacated opinion reported at 965 F.2d 80, 85-7 (6th Cir. 1992); United States v. Allison, 619 F.2d 1254, 1257 (8th Cir. 1980).

[124] United States v. Lartey, 716 F.2d 955, 962 (2d Cir. 1983)(evidence suggested that delay might well have resulted in the destruction or alteration of the subpoenaed records); United States v. Wilson, 614 F.2d 1224, 1228 (9th Cir. 1980)(evidence indicated that delay might have afforded an opportunity to forge documents); United States v. Triumph Capital Group, Inc, 211 F.R.D. 31, 55-56 (D.Conn. 2002)(exigent circumstances – the threat that evidence sought would be destroyed – justified use a forthwith grand jury subpoena).

[125] United States v. R. Enterprises, Inc., 498 U.S. 292, 301 (1991), quoting United States v. Mechanik, 475 U.S 66, 75 (1986)(O'Connor, J., concurring in the judgment); In re Grand Jury Proceedings, 115 F.3d 1240, 1244 (5th Cir. 1997); In re Grand Jury Subpoenas, 438 F.Supp.2d 111, 1120-121 (N.D.Cal. 2006).

[126] United States v. R. Enterprises, Inc., 498 U.S. 292, 299-301 (1992); In re Grand Jury, John Doe No. G.J. 2005-2, 478 F.3d 581, 585 (4th Cir. 2007)(internal citations omitted)("In the absence of such a privilege, a subpoena may still be unreasonable or oppressive under Rule 17(c) if it is irrelevant, harassing, overly vague, or excessively broad. Additionally, some courts have recognized that Rule 17(c) enables district courts to quash a subpoena that intrudes gravely on significant interests outside of the scope of a recognized privilege, if compliance is likely to entail consequences more serious than even severe inconveniences occasioned by irrelevant or overbroad request

for records"); In re Grand Jury Subpoenas, 906 F.2d 1485, 1496 (10th Cir. 1990); In re Grand Jury Subpoena Duces Tecum Dated November 15, 1993, 846 F.Supp. 11, 12-4 (S.D.N.Y. 1994)(quashing as overbroad a grand jury subpoena for all computer hard disk drives and floppy diskettes without any particular reference to their content). In R. Enterprises, the Court held that the party seeking to quash bears the burden of establishing that a particular subpoena is unreasonable because it is unduly burdensome or because of its want of specificity or relevancy and that a motion to quash on grounds of relevancy "must be denied unless there is no reasonable possibility that the category of materials the Government seeks will produce information relevant to the general subject of the grand jury's investigation." 498 U.S. at 301; In re Sealed Case (Espy), 121 F.3d 729, 759 (D.C.Cir. 1997); In re Grand Jury Subpoena, 175 F.3d 332, 339 (4th Cir. 1999); In re Green Grand Jury Proceedings, 371 F.Supp.2d 1055, 1057 (D.Minn. 2005). Here again, failure to comply with guidelines in the United States Attorneys' Manual or other internal directives will not per se render a grand jury subpoena subject to being quashed, In re Grand Jury Proceedings No.92-4, 42 F.3d 876, 880 (4th Cir. 1994).

[127] United States v. Dionisio, 410 U.S. 1 (1973).

[128] United States v. Mara, 410 U.S. 19 (1973).

[129] Doe v. United States, 487 U.S. 201 (1988).

[130] In re Green Grand Jury Proceedings, 371 F.Supp.2d 1055, 1056-58 (D.Minn. 2005); but see, In re Shabazz, 200 F.Supp.2d 578, 581-85 (D.S.C. 2002)(applying Fourth Amendment analysis to a motion to quash a grand jury subpoena duces tecum for a saliva sample sought for DNA testing purposes).

[131] ". . . [N]or shall any person . . . be compelled in any criminal case to be a witness against himself. . . ." U.S.Const. Amend.V.

[132] Cf., Griffin v. California, 380 U.S. 609, 613-14 (1965)(prosecutors are constitutionally barred from making uninvited comments on the defendants failure to testify to the jury); United States v. Garzon, 119 F.3d 1446, 1451 (10th Cir. 1997).

[133] United States v. Mandujano, 425 U.S. 564, 572 (1976). Nor is a witness entitled to Miranda warnings even if he or she is a target of the grand jury's investigation, 425 U.S. at 579; United States v. Byram, 145 F.3d 405, 409 (1st Cir. 1996); United States v. Gomez, 237 F.3d 238, 241-42 (3d Cir. 2000); United States v. Quam, 367 F.3d 1006, 1008 (8th Cir. 2004).

[134] United States v. Gomez, 237 F.3d 238, 240 (3d Cir. 2000). The Fifth Amendment, however, ordinarily does not permit a grand jury witness to refuse to answer on grounds his testimony will expose him to prosecution under foreign law, In re Grand Jury Proceedings of the Special April 2002 Grand Jury, 347 F.3d 197, 208 (7th Cir. 2003), citing, United States v. Balsys, 524 U.S. 666, 673-700 (7th Cir. 2003); United States v. Alvarez, 489 F.Supp.2d 714, 721-23 (W.D. Tex. 2007).

[135] United States v. Hubbell, 530 U.S. 27, 35-6 (2000), citing, Fisher v. United States, 425 U.S. 391, 409 (1976) and United States v. Doe, 465 U.S. 605, 612 (1984); In re Grand Jury Subpoena Dated April 18, 2003, 383 F.3d 905, 909 (9th Cir. 2004).

[136] United States v. Hubbell, 530 U.S. at 40-3; In re Grand Jury Witness, 92 F.3d 710, 712-13 (8th Cir. 1996); In re Grand Jury Subpoena Dated April 18, 2003, 383 F.3d 905, 909-10 (9th Cir. 2004).

[137] Braswell v. United States, 487 U.S. 99 (1988); cf., Bellis v. United States, 417 U.S.85 (1974)(upholding the contempt citation of an attorney for failure to comply with a grand jury subpoena for his law firm's business records); In re Grand Jury Witness, 92 F.3d 710, 712 (8th Cir. 1996).

[138] ". . .[N]or shall any person . . . be deprived of life, liberty, or property, without due process of law . . . ." U.S.Const. Amend. V.

[139] In re Green Grand Jury Proceedings, 492 F.3d 976, (8th Cir. 2007)("The government may not use the grand jury's investigative powers for the sole or dominant purpose of a preparing a pending indictment for trial. If the grand jury proceedings are directed toward other charges or persons, its scope cannot be narrowly circumscribed and any collateral fruits from bona fine inquires may be utilized by the government"); United States v. Anderson, 441 F.3d 1162, 1189 (10th Cir. 2006); United States v. Flemmi, 245 F.3d 24, 28 (1st Cir. 2001)("if a grand jury's continuing indagation results in the indictment of parties not previously charged, the presumption of regularity generally persists. So too when the grand jury's investigation leads to the filing of additional charges against previously indicted defendants"); United States v. Brothers Const. Co., 219 F.3d 300, 314 (4th Cir. 2000); United States v. Alred, 144 F.3d 1405, 1413 (11th Cir. 1998); cf., United States v. Salameh, 152 F.3d 88, 109 (2d Cir. 1998)("it is improper for the government to use a grand jury subpoena for the sole and dominant purpose of

preparing for trial, [under a pending indictment]. However, where there is some proper dominant purpose for the post-indictment subpoena the government is not barred from introducing evidence obtained thereby") (internal citations and quotation marks omitted).

[140] In re Grand Jury Subpoena Under Seal, 175 F.3d 332, 339-40 (4th Cir. 1999); In re Grand Jury Proceeding No.92-4, 42 F.3d 876, 878 (4th Cir. 1994); cf., United States v. Sells Engineering, Inc., 463 U.S. 418, 432 (1983)("If prosecutors in a given case knew that their colleagues would be free to use the materials generated by the grand jury in a civil case, they might be tempted to manipulate the grand jury's powerful investigative tools to root out additional evidence useful in the civil suit, or even to start or continue a grand jury inquiry where no criminal prosecution seemed likely. Any such use of grand jury proceedings to elicit evidence for use in a civil case is improper per se"). The attorney for the government, however, need not seek court approval to use the knowledge he gained by assisting in a grand jury in a related civil matter, United States v. John Doe, Inc., 481 U.S. 102 (1987).

[141] U.S. Const. Art.I, §6, cl.2.

[142] United States v. Rostenkowski, 59 F.3d 1291, 1300 (D.C.Cir. 1995); United States v. Swindall, 971 F.2d 1531, 1543 (11th Cir. 1992).

[143] "Whenever any wire or oral communications has been intercepted, no part of the contents of such communication and no evidence derived therefrom may be received in evidence . . . before . . . any grand jury . . . if the disclosure of that information would be in violation of this chapter [18 U.S.C. 2510-2522]." 18 U.S.C. 2515.

[144] Gelbard v. United States, 408 U.S. 41 (1971); In re Grand Jury Proceedings, Doe, 988 F.2d 211, 213 (1st Cir. 1992); In re Grand Jury, 111 F.3d 1066, 1077-79 (3d Cir. 1997); In re Grand Jury Investigation (John Doe), 437 F.3d 855, 857 (9th Cir. 2006).

[145] In re Grand Jury Proceedings (Kinamon), 45 F.3d 343, 347-48 (9th Cir. 1995) (interpreting 18 U.S.C. 6002).

[146] For instance one court has suggested that a grand jury subpoena does not constitute "court order" sufficient to trigger the exception to the confidentiality requirements of the Privacy Act, 5 U.S.C. 552a, with respect to records maintained by the federal government, Doe v. DiGenova, 779 F.2d 74, 85 (D.C.Cir. 1985), while another court has reached a contrary conclusion, In re Grand Jury Subpoena Issued to the United States Postal Service, 535 F.Supp. 31, 32-33 (E.D.Tenn. 1981). In the course of its opinion the Doe court noted a similar

divergence of views on the question of whether a grand jury subpoena constituted a court order sufficient to trigger an exception in the Fair Credit Reporting Act (15 U.S.C. 1681), Doe, 779 F.2d at 81 n.16 citing In re Grand Jury Subpoena Duces Tecum Concerning Credit Bureau, Inc., 498 F.Supp. 1174 (N.D.Ga. 1980) and in re Application of Credit Information Corp. of New York to Quash Grand Jury Subpoena, 526 F.Supp. 1253 (D.Md. 1981), in contrast to, In re Grand Jury Proceedings, 503 F.Supp. 9 (D.N.J. 1980) and In re Subpoena Duces Tecum to Testify Before Grand Jury Directed to TRW, Inc., 460 F.Supp. 1007 (E.D.Mich. 1978); compare also, United States v. 218 3rd St., 805 F.2d 256, 60-62 (7th Cir. 1986), with In re Castiglione, 587 F.Supp. 1210 (E.D.Cal. 1984), with respect to exceptions to the confidentiality requirements of the Right to Financial Privacy Act (12 U.S.C. 3420). In re August, 1993 Regular Grand Jury, 854 F.Supp. 1380, 1382-385 (S.D.Ind. 1994) recognizes the authority to quash a grand jury subpoena to preserve the confidentiality of hospital records concerning drug abuse treatment patients under 42 U.S.C. 290dd-2.

[147] In re Grand Jury Proceedings No. 92-4, 42 F.3d 876, 880 (4th Cir. 1994); In re Grand Jury Proceedings (Chesnoff), 13 F.3d 1293, 1296 (9th Cir. 1994).

[148] Compare, Whitehouse v. United States District Court, 53 F.3d 1349 (1st Cir. 1995), with, Stern v. United States District Court, 214 F.3d 4 (1st Cir. 2000).

[149] ". . . The following persons may be present while the grand jury is in session: attorneys for the government, the witness being questioned, interpreters when needed, and a court reporter or an operator of a recording device . . . No person other than the jurors, and any interpreter needed to assist a hearing-impaired or speech-impaired juror, may be present while the grand jury is deliberating or voting." F.R.Crim.P. 6(d).

[150] "(A) No obligation of secrecy may be imposed on any person except in accordance with Rule 6(e)(2)(B). (B) Unless these rules provide otherwise, the following persons must not disclose a matter occurring before the grand jury: (i) a grand juror; (ii) an interpreter; (iii) a court reporter; (iv) an operator of a recording device; (v) a person who transcribes recorded testimony; (vi) an attorney for the government; or (vii) a person to whom disclosure is made under Rule 6(e)(3)(A)(ii) or (iii). . .(7) Contempt. A knowing violation of Rule 6, or of guidelines jointly issued by the Attorney General and

the Director of National Intelligence pursuant to Rule 6, may be punished as a contempt of court." F.R.Crim.P. 6(e)(2),(7).

[151] United States v. Sells Engineering, Inc., 463 U.S. 418, 424 (1983), quoting, Douglas Oil Co. v. Petrol Stops Northwest, 441 U.S. 211, 218 (1979).

[152] United States v. John Doe, Inc., 481 U.S. 102, 109 n.5 (1987), quoting United States v. Rose, 215 F.2d 617, 628-29 (3d Cir. 1954) and United States v. Procter and Gamble Co., 356 U.S. 677, 681-82 n.6. (1958); Douglas Oil Co. v. Petrol Stops Northwest, 441 U.S. 211, 219 n.10 (1979). Douglas Oil Co. offered an alternative formulation, "First, if preindictment proceedings were made public, many prospective witnesses would be hesitant to come forward voluntarily, knowing that those against whom they testify would be aware of that testimony. Moreover, witnesses who appeared before the grand jury would be less likely to testify fully and frankly, as they would be open to retribution as well as to inducements. There also would be the risk that those about to be indicted would flee, or would try to influence individual grand jurors to vote against indictment. Finally, by preserving the secrecy of the proceedings, we assure that persons who are accused but exonerated by the grand jury will not be held up to public ridicule," Douglas Oil Co. v. Petrol Stops Northwest, 441 U.S. at 219. The two are obviously similar and subsequent lower court decisions seem to show no real preference, Douglas Oil Co. formula, In re Grand Jury Subpoena, Judith Miller, 493 F.3d 152, 154 (D.C. Cir. 2007); United States v. Aisenberg, 358 F.3d 1327 (11th Cir. 2004)(citing Douglas Oil); In re Newark Morning Ledger Co., 260 F.3d 217, 221 (3d Cir. 2001)(same); Camiolo v. State Farm Fire and Cas.Co., 334 F.3d 345, 355 (3d Cir. 2003)(citing Rose); In re Petition of Craig, 131 F.3d 99, 102 (2d Cir. 1997)(same).

[153] Douglas Oil Co. v. Petrol Stops Northwest, 441 U.S. 211, 218-19 (1979)("disclosure is appropriate only in those cases where the need for it outweighs the public interest in secrecy"); United Kingdom v. United States, 238 F.3d 1312, 1320 (11th Cir. 2001).

[154] F.R.Crim.P. 6(e)(2).

[155] United States v. Sells Engineering, Inc., 463 U.S. 418, 425 (1983)("Witnesses are not under the prohibition unless they also happen to fit into one of the enumerated classes [e.g., grand juror, interpreter, court reporter, attorney for the government, etc.]"); Butterworth v. Smith, 494 U.S. 624 (1990)(holding unconstitutional,

as a violation of the First Amendment, a Florida statute that prohibited a witness from ever disclosing his or her grand jury testimony); cf., In re Sealed Motion, 880 F.2d 1367, 1373 (D.C. Cir. 1989)(holding that "a grand jury witness has a general right to a transcript of [his or her own] testimony absent the government demonstrating countervailing interests which outweigh the right to release of a transcript")(contra, In re Grand Jury Subpoena, 72 F.3d 271, 275-76 (2d Cir. 1995), (holding that grand jury witnesses do not have a presumptive right to a copy of their grand jury testimony on demand); In re Grand Jury Proceedings, 417 F.3d 18, 25-8 (1st Cir. 2005)(holding that under narrow circumstances the inherent power of the court to impose secrecy orders incidental to the matters occurring before them includes the power to impose such orders upon grand jury witnesses).

[156] Fund for Constitutional Government v. National Archives, 656 F.2d 856, 870 n.33 (D.C. Cir. 1981); United States v. Forman, 71 F.3d 1214, 1217-220 (6th Cir. 1995); In re Polyprophylene Carpet Antitrust Litigation, 181 F.R.D. 680, 692-94 (N.D.Ga. 1998); Beale et al., GRAND JURY LAW AND PRACTICE §5.4 (1998). Under some circumstances, however, such disclosures may constitute violations of 18 U.S.C. 641 (theft of federal property) or 1503 (obstruction of justice), see United States v. Jeter, 775 F.2d 670 (6th Cir. 1985) (upholding convictions under both sections of a defendant who had sold information, obtained from carbon paper used to type transcripts of grand jury proceedings, to the targets of the grand jury investigations).

[157] F.R.Crim.P. 6(e)(2)(B); see generally, What Are "Matters Occurring Before the Grand Jury" Within Prohibition of Rule 6(e) of the Federal Rules of Criminal Procedure, 50 ALR Fed 675; FRCrP 6(e) and the Disclosure of Documents Reviewed by a Grand Jury, 57 UNIVERSITY OF CHICAGO LAW REVIEW 221 (1990); 1 Beale et al., GRAND JURY LAW AND PRACTICE §5.6 (1998).

[158] United States v. Eastern Air Lines, Inc., 923 F.2d 241, 244 (2d Cir. 1991); but see, In re Motions of Dow Jones and Co., 142 F.3d 496, 500 (D.C.Cir. 1998)("The phrase — 'matters occurring before the grand jury''— includes not only what has occurred and what is occurring, but also what is like to occur"); In re Cudahy, 294 F.3d 947, 951(7th Cir. 2002))("the purpose of Rule 6(e) is to protect the confidentiality of the grand jury's hearings and deliberations, and the term matters occurring before the grand jury is interpreted

accordingly. See Martin v. Consultants and Administrators, Inc., 966 F.2d 1078, 1097 (7th Cir. 1992)('the general rule is that Rule 6(e)'s nondisclosure requirement applies to anything that may reveal what occurred before the grand jury'); In re Sealed Case No. 99-3091, 192 F.2d 995, 1001 (D.C.Cir. 1999)(the phrase matters occurring before the grand jury encompasses 'not only what has occurred and what is occurring, but also what is likely to occur, including the identities of witnesses or jurors, the substance of testimony as well as actual transcripts, the strategy or direction of the investigation, the deliberations or questions of jurors, and the like'); United States v. Phillips, 843 F.2d 438, 441 (11th Cir. 1988)('the term matter occurring before the gand jury has been defined to include anything that will reveal what transpired during the grand jury proceedings'); Standley v. Department of Justice, 835 F.2d 216, 218 (9th Cir. 1987))('anything which may reveal what occurred before the grand jury' or 'information which would reveal the identities of witnesses or jurors, the substance of testimony, the strategy or direction of the investigation, the deliberations or questions of the jurors, and the like')").

[159] See e.g., United States v. Dynavac, Inc., 6 F.3d 1407, 1411-414 (9th Cir. 1993), which first notes that "Rule 6(e) is intended only to protect against disclosure of what is said or takes place in the grand jury room . . . it is not the purpose of the Rule to foreclose from all future revelations to proper authorities the same information or documents which were presented to the grand jury. Thus, if a document is sought for its own sake rather than to learn what took place before the grand jury, and if its disclosure will not compromise the integrity of the grand jury process, Rule 6(e) does not prohibit its release." The Dynavac court then goes on to discuss the several, various different tests used by other circuits to determine when business records subpoena by the grand jury should be considered covered by Rule 6(e); see also, In re Grand Jury Investigation (Missouri), 55 F.3d 350, 353-54 (8th Cir. 1995); Kersting v. United States, 206 F.3d 817, 821 (9th Cir. 2000)("The law, however, is clear that business records sought for intrinsic value are admissible, even if the same documents were also presented to the grand jury. The only exception . . . is if the material reveals a secret aspect of the grand jury's workings"); In re Cudahy, 294 F.3d 947, 952 (7th Cir. 2002)("these formulations do not suggest that the mere fact of the existence of a grand jury is automatically to be deemed a matter

occurring before it. . . unless revelation of its existence would disclose the identities of the targets or subjects of the grand jury's investigation").

[160] "(5) Closed Hearing. Subject to any right to an open hearing in a contempt proceeding, the court must close any hearing to the extent necessary to prevent disclosure of a matter occurring before a grand jury. "(6) Sealed Records. Records, orders, and subpoenas relating to grand jury proceedings must be kept under seal to the extent and as long as necessary to prevent disclosure of a matter occurring before a grand jury," F.R.Crim.P. 6(e)(5), (6). These provisions have withstood First Amendment challenges in at least three circuits, In re Newark Morning Ledger Co., 260 F.3d 217 (3d Cir. 2001); In re Motions of Dow Jones and Co., 142 F.3d 496 (D.C.Cir. 1998); In re Grand Jury Subpoena (John Doe No. 4), 103 F.3d 234 (2d Cir. 1996).

[161] In re Grand Jury, Judith Miller, 493 F.3d 152, 154 (D.C. Cir. 2007)(internal quotation marks omitted).

[162] United States v. John Doe, Inc. I, 481 U.S. 102 (1987). But individual use may not include disclosure to the court before whom the civil litigation is pending without prior judicial approval, In re Sealed Case (Qui Tam), 250 F.3d 764, 768 (D.C.Cir. 2001)("The Government . . . takes the untenable and disturbingly cavalier position a sealed, ex parte, conveyance of grand jury information to a federal who is acting in his judicial capacity is not a disclosure within the meaning to the grand jury secrecy rule").

[163] "(A) Disclosure of a grand-jury matter – other than the grand jury's deliberations or any grand juror's vote – may be made to: (i) an attorney for the government for use in performing that attorney's duty; (ii) any government personnel – including those of a state, state subdivision, Indian tribe, or foreign government – that an attorney for the government considers necessary to assist in performing that attorney's duty to enforce federal criminal law; or (iii) a person authorized by 18 U.S.C. § 3322 [relating to the disclosure of grand jury matters to government attorneys in civil forfeiture cases and with court approval to bank regulatory agencies in certain cases]. "(B) A person to whom information is disclosed under Rule 6(e)(3)(A)(ii) may use that information only to assist an attorney for the government in performing that attorney's duty to enforce federal criminal law. An attorney for the government must promptly provide the court that impaneled the grand jury with the names of all persons

to whom a disclosure has been made, and must certify that the attorney has advised those persons of their obligation of secrecy under this rule." F.R.Crim.P. 6(e)(3)(A), (B).

[164] United States v. Sells Engineering, Inc., 463 U.S. 418, 427 (1983) ("The Government contends that all attorneys in the Justice Department qualify for automatic disclosure of grand jury materials under (A)(i), regardless of the nature of the litigation in which they intend to use the materials. We hold that (A)(i) disclosure is limited to use by those attorneys who conduct the criminal matters to which the materials pertain").

[165] In re November 1992 Special Grand Jury for the Northern District of Indiana, 836 F.Supp. 615, 616-17 (N.D.Ind. 1993); but see, United States v. Pimental, 380 F.3d 575, 591-96 (1st Cir. 2004)(holding that investigators of a "hybrid private/public" insurance association should be considered government personnel for grand jury disclosure purposes).

[166] "(D) An attorney for the government may disclose any grand-jury matter involving foreign intelligence, counterintelligence (as defined in 50 U.S.C. § 401a), or foreign intelligence information (as defined in Rule 6(e)(3)(D)(iii)) to any federal law enforcement, intelligence, protective, immigration, national defense, or national security official to assist the official receiving the information in the performance of that official's duties. An attorney for the government may also disclose any grand jury matter involving, within the United States or elsewhere, a threat of attack or other grave hostile acts of a foreign power or its agent, a threat of domestic or international sabotage or terrorism, or clandestine intelligence gathering activities by an intelligence service or network of a foreign power or by its agent, to any appropriate Federal, State, State subdivision, Indian tribal, or foreign government official, for the purpose of preventing or responding to such threat or activities. "(i) Any official who receives information under Rule 6(e)(3)(D) may use the information only as necessary in the conduct of that person's official duties subject to any limitations on the unauthorized disclosure of such information. Any State, State subdivision, Indian tribal, or foreign government official who receives information under Rule 6(e)(3)(D) may use the information only consistent with such guidelines issued by the Attorney General and the Director of National Intelligence. "(ii) Within a reasonable time after disclosure is made under Rule 6(e)(3)(D), an attorney for the government must file, under seal, a

notice with the court in the district where the grand jury convened stating that such information was disclosed and the departments, agencies, or entities to which the disclosure was made. "(iii) As used in Rule 6(e)(3)(D), the term "foreign intelligence information" means: (a) information, whether or not it concerns a United States person, that relates to the ability of the United States to protect against – [1] actual or potential attack or other grave hostile acts of a foreign power or its agent; [2] sabotage or international terrorism by a foreign power or its agent; or [3] clandestine intelligence activities by an intelligence service or network of a foreign power or by its agent; or (b) information, whether or not it concerns a United States person, with respect to a foreign power or foreign territory that relates to –[1] the national defense or the security of the United States; or [2] the conduct of the foreign affairs of the United States." F.R.Crim.P. 6(e)(3)(D). See generally, Shaw, The USA PATRIOT Act of 2001, the Intelligence Reform and Terrorism Prevention Act of 2004, and the False Dichotomy Between Protecting National Security and Preserving Grand Jury Secrecy, 35 SETON HALL LAW REVIEW 495 (2005); Collins, And the Walls Came Tumbling Down: Sharing Grand Jury Information with the Intelligence Community Under the USA PATRIOT Act, 39 AMERICAN CRIMINAL LAW REVIEW 1261 (2002).

[167] "(E) The court may authorize disclosure – at a time, in a manner, and subject to any other conditions that it directs – of a grand jury matter: (i) preliminary to or in connection with a judicial proceeding," F.R.Crim.P. 6(e)(3)(E)(i).

[168] Doe v. Rosenbery, 225 F.2d 118 (2d Cir. 1958); In re Special February 1977 Grand Jury v. Conlisk, 490 F.2d 894 (7th Cir. 1973).

[169] United States v. Shillitani, 345 F.2d 290 (2d Cir. 1965).

[170] Gibson v. United States, 403 F.3d 166 (D.C.Cir. 1968).

[171] Haldeman v. Sirica, 501 F.2d 714 (D.C.Cir. 1974)(impeach inquiry); In re Grand Jury Investigation of Ven-Fuel, 441 F.Supp. 1299 (M.D.Fla. 1977)(legislative investigation).

[172] In re Grand Jury Proceedings (Daewoo), 613 F.Supp. 673 (D.Ore. 1985)(Customs Service proceedings).

[173] In re Grand Jury Investigation, 414 F.Supp. 74 (S.D.N.Y. 1976).

[174] In re 1979 Grand Jury Proceedings, 479 F.Supp. 93 (E.D.N.Y. 1973).

[175] Interestingly, (C)(i),(now (E)(i)) might have permitted disclosure in Baggot if the tax payer, rather than the IRS, had sought disclosure in

anticipation of a judicial challenge of the results of the audit: "Of course, the matter may end up in court if Baggot chooses to take it there, but that possibility does not negate the fact that the primary use to which the IRS purposes to put the materials it seeks is an extrajudicial one – the assessment of a tax deficiency by the IRS," 463 at 481.

[176] 463 U.S. at 479 n.2; the D.C. Circuit subsequently found the exception extended to the proceedings conducted to determine the extent to which final reports of Independent Counsels should be made public, In re North, 16 F.3d 1234, 1244-245 (D.C.Cir. 1989); In re Espy, 259 F.3d 725, 728 (D.C.Cir. 2001), and to subsequent grand jury proceedings, In re Grand Jury, 490 F.3d 978, 986 (D.C. Cir. 2007)(citing various circuit court views on whether a grand jury witness should be permitted to examine or copy his testimony).

[177] 463 U.S. at 480-81 n.5.

[178] United States v. Sells Engineering, Inc., 463 U.S. at 443; Right of Party in Civil Action to Obtain Disclosure, Under Rule 6(e)(3)(C)(i) of the Federal Rules of Criminal Procedure, of Matters Occurring Before Grand Jury, 71 ALR FED 10.

[179] Douglas Oil Co. v. Northwest Petrol Stops, 441 U.S. at 222; United States v. Moussaoui, 483 F.3d 220, 235 (4th Cir. 2007); United States v. Aisenberg, 358 F.3d 1327, 1348 (11th Cir. 2004); McAninch v. Wintermute, 491 F.3d 759, 767 (8th Cir. 2007); United States v. Campbell, 324 F.3d 497, 498-99 (7th Cir. 2003); In re Special Grand Jury 89-2, 143 F.3d 565, 569-70 (10th Cir. 1998); In re Grand Jury Proceedings (Ballas), 62 F.3d 1175, 1179 (9th Cir. 1995); United States v. Miramontex, 995 F.2d 56, 59 (5th Cir. 1993).

[180] In re Grand Jury 95-1, 118 F.3d 1433, 1437 (10th Cir. 1997); In re Grand Jury Investigation (Missouri), 55 F.3d 350, 354-55 (8th Cir. 1995); Cullen v. Margiotta, 811 F.2d 698, 715 (2d Cir. 1987); Hernly v. United States, 832 F.2d 980, 883-85 (7th Cir. 1987); In re Grand Jury Proceedings GJ-76-4 and GJ-75-3, 800 F.2d 1293, 1302 (4th Cir. 1986).

[181] United States v. John Doe, Inc.I, 481 U.S. 102, 112 (1987); citing, United States v. Sells Engineering, Inc., 463 U.S. 418, 443-44 (1983); and Illinois v. Abbott and Associates, Inc., 460 U.S. 557 (1983).

[182] United States v. John Doe, Inc. I, 481 U.S. at 112; cf., In re Grand Jury Investigation (Missouri), 55 F.3d 350, 353-54 (8th Cir. 1995).

[183] Douglas Oil Co.v. Northwest Petrol Stops, 441 U.S. at 222; United States v. Nix, 21 F.3d 347, 351 (9th Cir. 1994).

[184] In re Grand Jury Proceedings (Ballas), 62 F.3d 1175, 1180 (9th Cir. 1995); United States v. Aisenberg, 358 F.3d 1327, 1349 (11th Cir. 2004).

[185] United States v. Socony-Vacuum Oil Co., 310 U.S. 150, 234 (1940); In re Grand Jury Investigation (Missouri), 55 F.3d 380, 354 (8th Cir. 1995); In re Grand Jury Proceeding Relative to Perl, 838 F.2d 304, 307 (8th Cir. 1988).

[186] United States v. Blackwell, 954 F.Supp. 944, 966 (D.N.J. 1997); In re Grand Jury Proceedings GJ-76-4 and GJ-75-3, 800 F.2d at 1301 (4th Cir. 1986); In re Shopping Cart Antitrust Litigation, 95 F.R.D. 309, 312-13 (S.D.N.Y. 1982).

[187] United States v. Aisenberg, 358 F.3d 1327, 1348 (11th Cir. 2004); Hernly v. United States, 832 F.2d 980, 985 (7th Cir. 1987); In re Grand Jury Testimony, 832 F.2d 60, 64 (5th Cir. 1987).

[188] Cullen v. Margiotta, 811 F.2d 698 (2d Cir. 1987); In re Grand Jury Investigation (Missouri), 55 F.3d 350, 355 (8th Cir. 1955).

[189] In re Grand Jury Proceeding Relative to Perl, 838 F.2d 304, 306-307 (8th Cir. 1988); In re Grand Jury Investigation (Missouri), 55 F.3d at 354 (8th Cir. 1995); In re Sealed Case, 801 F.2d 1379, 1381 (D.C.Cir. 1986); In re Grand Jury Investigation, 630 F.2d 996, 1000 (3d Cir. 1980).

[190] Douglas Oil Co., 441 U.S. at 222 n.12; United States v. Rockwell International Corp., 173 F.3d 757, 759 (10th Cir. 1999); In re Grand Jury, 832 F.2d 60, 63 (5th Cir. 1987); Lucas v. Turner, 725 F.2d 1095, 1105 (7th Cir. 1984); United States v. Fischbach and Moore, Inc., 776 F.2d 839, 845 (9th Cir. 1985). Under much the same logic, a court may afford a grand jury witness access to his or her earlier testimony prior to a subsequent appearance, In re Grand Jury, 490 F.3d 978, 986-90 (D.C. Cir. 2007).

[191] Douglas Oil Co., 441 U.S. at 222 n.13; In re Grand Jury Proceedings GJ-76-4 and GJ-75-3, 800 F.2d 1293, 1302-303 (4th Cir. 1986); United States v. Fischbach and Moore, Inc., 776 F.2d 839, 844 (9th Cir. 1985).

[192] "(E) The court may authorize disclosure – at a time, in a manner, and subject to any other conditions that it directs – of a grand jury matter: . . . (ii) at the request of a defendant who shows that a ground may exist to dismiss the indictment because of a matter that occurred before the grand jury." F.R.Crim.P. 6(e)(3)(E)(ii).

[193] United States v. Wilkinson, 124 F.3d 971, 977 (8th Cir. 1997); United States v. Perez, 67 F.3d 1371, 1381 (9th Cir. 1995); United States v. Puglia, 8 F.3d 478, 480 (7th Cir. 1993); United States v. Miramontez, 995 F.2d 56, 59 (5th Cir. 1993); United States v. Gibson, 175 F.Supp.2d 532, 535 (S.D.N.Y. 2001).

[194] "(C) An attorney for the government may disclose any grand jury matter to another federal grand jury." F.R.Crim.P. 6(e)(3)(C).

[195] In re Grand Jury Subpoenas Aug. 1986, 658 F.Supp. 474, 478-80 (D.Md. 1987).

[196] "(E) The court may authorize disclosure – at a time, in a manner, and subject to any other conditions that it directs – of a grand jury matter: . . . (iii) at the request of the government, when sought by a foreign court or prosecutor for use in an official criminal investigation; (iv) at the request of the government if it shows that the matter may disclose a violation of state, Indian tribal, or foreign criminal law, as long as the disclosure is to an appropriate state, state-subdivision, Indian trial, or foreign government official for the purpose of enforcing that law; (v) at the request of the government if it shows that the matter may disclose a violation of military criminal law under the Uniform Code of Military Justice, as long as the disclosure is to an appropriate military official for the purpose of enforcing that law," F.R.Crim.P. 6(e)(3)(E)(iii), (iv),(v).

[197] United States v. McVeigh, 157 F.3d 809, 814-15 (10th Cir. 1998).

[198] F.R.Crim.P. 16(a)(1)(A).

[199] 18 U.S.C. 3500; see also F.R.Crim.P. 26.2.

[200] 18 U.S.C. 3322.

[201] Illinois v. Abbott and Associates, Inc., 460 U.S. 557 (1983); see also, In re North, 16 F.3d 1234, 1243 (D.C.Cir. 1994) holding that the statutory obligation of Independent Counsel to submit a final report of their investigations and prosecutions, 28 U.S.C. 585(b), did not relieve them of the obligations of government attorneys under Rule 6(e).

[202] In re Grand Jury Investigation (John Doe), 59 F.3d 17, 19-20 (2d Cir. 1995)(permitting access to documents held by the grand jury when sought in response to the legitimate needs of the entity that created the documents); In re Report and Recommendation of June 5, 1972 Grand Jury, 370 F.Supp. 1219, 1227-230 (D.D.C. 1974) (permitting disclosure of grand jury material relevant to an impeachment inquiry to the House Judiciary Committee); In re Grand Jury Investigation of Ven-Fuel, 441 F.Supp. 1299, 1302-304

(M.D.Fla. 1977) (permitting disclosure of grand jury material a House legislative subcommittee); In re Petition to Inspect and Copy Grand Jury Materials, 735 F.2d 1261, 1270 (11th Cir. 1984)(upholding disclosure of grand jury matter to an committee of the Eleventh Circuit Judicial Council investigating allegations of judicial misconduct on the grounds of the district court's inherent supervisory power over the grand jury). The Second Circuit offered a "non-exclusive list of factors that a trial court might want to consider when confronted with these highly discretionary and fact-sensitive special circumstance motions [for disclosure of grand jury information on grounds other than those specified in Rule 6(e)(3)]: (i) the identity of the party seeking disclosure; (ii) whether the defendant to the grand jury proceeding or the government opposes the disclosure; (iii) why disclosure is being sought in the particular case; (iv) what specific information is being sought for disclosure; (v) how long ago the grand jury proceeding took place; (vii) the current status of the principals of the grand jury proceedings and that of their families; (vii) the extent to which the desired material — either permissibly or impermissibly — has been previously made public; (viii) whether witnesses to the grand jury proceedings who might be affected by disclosure are still alive; and (ix) the additional need for maintaining secrecy in the particular case in question," In re Petition of Craig, 131 F.3d 99, 106 (2d Cir. 1997).

[203] In re Grand Jury Subpoena (John Doe No.4), 103 F.3d 234, 240 n.8 (2d Cir. 1996); In re Grand Jury Proceedings, 417 F.3d 18, 26 (1st Cir. 2006); In re Charlotte Observer, 921 F.2d 47, 50 (4th Cir. 1990), citing, Matter of Special March 1981 Grand Jury, 753 F.2d 575, 577 (7th Cir. 1985); In re Subpoena to Testify Before Grand Jury, 864 F.2d 1559, 1563-64 (11th Cir. 1989); see also, In re Special Grand Jury, 450 F.3d 1159, 1177-178 (10th Cir. 2006)(noting the authority in other circuits but postponing consideration of the question).

[204] F.R.Crim.P. 6(e)(7)("A knowing violation of Rule 6, or of the guidelines jointly issued by the Attorney General and the Director of National Intelligence under Rule 6, may be punished as a contempt of court"); Bank of Nova Scotia v. United States, 487 U.S. at 263; United States v. Holloway, 991 F.2d 370 (7th Cir. 1993); Relief, Remedy, or Sanction for Violation of Rule 6(e) of Federal Rules of Criminal Procedure Prohibiting Disclosure of Matters Occurring Before Grand Jury, 73 ALR FED 112.

[205] McQueen v. Bullock, 907 F.2d 1544, 1551 (5th Cir. 1990); In re Grand Jury Investigation (Lance), 610 F.2d 202, 213 (5th Cir. 1980); Barry v. United States, 865 F.2d 1317 (D.C.Cir. 1989); contra, In re Grand Jury Investigation (90-3-2), 748 F.Supp. 1188 (E.D. Mich. 1990). The Eleventh Circuit panel in Blalock v. United States, 844 F.2d 1546 (11th Cir. 1988), felt itself bound by precedent of the Fifth Circuit before that circuit was split in two to create the Eleventh and Fifth, but two of the three members of the panel make it clear that they would have held otherwise if not bound, 844 F.2d at 1551-553 (Tjoflat and Roettger, JJ. concurring). See generally, Federal Rule of Criminal Procedure 6(e): Criminal or Civil Contempt for Violations of Grand Jury Secrecy?, 12 WESTERN NEW ENGLAND LAW REVIEW 245 (1990).

[206] Bank of Nova Scotia v. United States, 487 U.S. at 263. The civil relief available against government for violations of grand jury secrecy does not include the right to monetary damages or attorneys' fees, In re Sealed Case, No. 98-3077, 151 F.3d 1059, 1070 (D.C.Cir. 1998); McQueen v. United States, 5 F.Supp.2d 473, 482-83 (S.D.Tex. 1998).

[207] United States v. Jeter, 775 F.2d 670, 675-79 (6th Cir. 1985); United States v. Howard, 569 F.2d 1331, 1336 (5th Cir. 1978); United States v. Peasley, 741 F.Supp. 18, 20 (D.Me. 1990); In re Grand Jury Proceedings, Special Grand Jury 89-2, 813 F.Supp. 1451, 1465 n.10 (D.Colo. 1992).

[208] F.R.Crim.P. 7(c)(1), 6(c). The foreperson's failure to endorse the indictment is not fatal unless it reflects the absence of a concurrence of twelve grand jurors in the indictment, Hobby v. United States, 468 U.S. 339, 345 (1984), citing, Frisbie v. United States, 157 U.S. 160, 163-65 (1895). The signature or assent of the attorney for the government, however, is required before a prosecution can go forward, United States v. Cox, 342 F.2d 167, 171-72 (5th Cir. 1965); United States v. Laboy, 909 F.2d 581, 585 (1st Cir. 1990).

[209] United States v. Resendiz-Ponce, 127 S.Ct. 782,788 (2007); United States v. Abu-Shawish, 507 F.3d 550, 553 (7th Cir. 2007); United States v. Kemp, 500 F.3d 257, 280 (3d Cir. 2007); United States v. Ratcliff, 488 F.3d 639, 643 (5th Cir. 2007).

[210] "No person shall be held to answer for a capital, or otherwise infamous crime, unless on a presentment or indictment of a grand jury. . . ." U.S. Const. Amend. V; Stirone v. United States, 361 U.S. 212, 215-19 (1960); United States v. Doe, 297 F.3d 76, 88 n,12 (2d

Cir. 2002); United States v. Adamson, 291 F.3d 606, 614 (9th Cir. 2002); United States v. Weiss, 469 F.Supp.2d 941, 945 (D. Colo. 2007).

[211] F.R.Crim.P. 7(b); Ornelas v. United States, 840 F.2d 890, 892 n.3 (11th Cir. 1988); United States v. Moore, 37 F.3d 169, 173 (5th Cir. 1995); cf., United States v. Littlefield, 105 F.3d 527, 528 (9th Cir. 1997); Goode v. United States, 305 F.3d 378, 386 (6th Cir. 2002); United States v. Stewart, 425 F.Supp.2d 727, 736 (E.D. Va. 2006).

[212] F.R.Crim.P. 7(a); United States v. Brewer, 681 F.2d 973, 974 (5th Cir. 1982); United States v. Cocoman, 903 F.2d 127, 129-30 (2d Cir. 1990); United States v. Pitt-Des Moines, Inc., 168 F.3d 976, 986 (7th Cir. 1999); United States v. Greenpeace, Inc., 314 F.Supp.2d 1252, 1264 (S.D.Fla. 2004).

[213] F.R.Crim.P. 6(f); United States v. Byron, 994 F.2d 747, 748 (10th Cir. 1993), but some courts have held that the requirement is not jurisdictional and may be waived or, if harmless, provides inadequate grounds to vacate a conviction, United States v. Enigwe, 17 F.Supp.2d 390, 392 (E.D.Pa. 1998).

[214] United States v. Calandra, 414 U.S. 338, 343 (1974), citing Branzburg v. Hayes, 408 U.S. 665, 686-87 (1972); United States v. Cabrera-Teran, 168 F.3d 141, 143 (5th Cir. 1999).

[215] Bank of Nova Scotia v. United States, 487 U.S. 250, 257 (1988); Vasquez v. Hillary, 474 U.S. 254, 260-64 (1986).

[216] United States v. Mayer, 503 F.3d 740, 747 (9th Cir. 2007); In re Sealed Case (No. 98-3054), 144 F.3d 74, 75 (D.C.Cir. 1998); United States v. Nanni, 59 F.3d 1425, 1432-433 (2d Cir. 1995); Grand Jury Subpoena Dated Dec. 7 and 8, 40 F.3d 1096, 1103 (10th Cir. 1994); In re Grand Jury Proceedings (Kinamon), 45 F.3d 343, 347-48 (9th Cir. 1995); but see, United States v. Schmidgall, 25 F.3d 1533, 1538-539 (11th Cir. 1994)(disclosure of immunized testimony to an indicting grand jury does not require dismissal if the disclosure is shown to have been harmless).

[217] United States v. Mayer, 503 F.3d 740, 747 (9th Cir. 2007); United States v. Cochran, 17 F.3d 56, 57 (3d Cir. 1994), citing, United States v. Russell, 369 U.S. 749, 763-64 (1962); United States v. Brown, 995 F.2d 1493, 1505 (10th Cir. 1993). Indictments defective on their face may include those returned after the expiration of the grand jury's tenure, but whether apparent from the face of the indictment or not a purported indictment returned by a grand jury's whose term has expired is a nullity, United States v. Fein, 504 F.2d

1170, 1173 (2d Cir. 1974); United States v. Armored Transport Inc., 629 F.2d 1313, 1316 (9th Cir. 1980); United States v. Clemenic, 886 F.2d 332 (7th Cir. 1989), opinion appended to United States v. Daniels, 902 F.2d 1238, 1240 (7th Cir. 1990).

[218] United States v. Swindall, 971 F.2d 1531, 1543 (11th Cir. 1992); United States v. Helstoski, 635 F.2d 200, 204-6 (3d Cir. 1980); cf., United States v. Rostenkowski, 59 F.3d 1291, 1298-299 (D.C.Cir. 1995)(noting that at some point presentation of speech or debate material to a grand jury will contaminate the resulting indictment but declining to identify that point).

[219] United States v. Stein, 495 F.3d 390, 421-25 (S.D.N.Y. 2007).

[220] United States v. MacDonald, 435 U.S. 850, 860 n.7 (1978), citing Abney v. United States, 431 U.S. 651, 663 (1977); Cogen v. United States, 278 U.S. 221, 227 (1920); and Heike v. United States, 217 U.S. 423, 430 (1910); United States v. Mayer, 503 F.3d 740, 747 (9th Cir. 2007).

[221] United States v. Mayer, 503 F.3d 740, 747 (9th Cir. 2007).

[222] United States v. Jennings, 991 F.2d 725, 730 (11th Cir. 1993)("In order to prevail in a selective prosecution defense, a defendant must meet the heavy burden of (1) making a prima facie showing that he has been singled out for prosecution although other similarly situated persons who have committed the same acts have not been prosecuted; and (2) demonstrate that the government's selective prosecution was unconstitutional because actuated by impermissible motives such as racial or religious discrimination"); cf., United States v. Estrada-Plata, 57 F.3d 757, 760 (9th Cir. 1995); United States v. Cooks, 52 F.3d 101, 105 (5th Cir. 1995); United States v. Mayer, 503 F.3d 740, 747 (9th Cir. 2007).

[223] United States v. Meyer, 810 F.2d 1242, 1249 (D.C.Cir. 1987), vac'd, 816 F. 2d 695, reinstated, 824 F.2d 1240; cf., United States v. Cyprian, 23 F.3d 1189, 1196 (7th Cir. 1994)("prosecution is vindictive, in violation of the Fifth Amendment Due Process Clause, if it is undertaken in retaliation for the exercise of a legally protected statutory or constitutional right"); United States v. Aggarwal, 17 F.3d 737, 743-44 (5th Cir. 1994).

[224] United States v. Mayer, 503 F.3d 740, 747 (9th Cir. 2007), citing, United States v. Russell, 411 U.S. 423, 432 (1973); United States v. Montoya, 45 F.3d 1286, 1300 (9th Cir. 1995); cf., United States v. Sneed, 34 F.3d 1570, 1576-578 (10th Cir. 1994); United States v. LaPorta, 46 F.3d 152, 160 (2d Cir. 1994).

[225] United States v. Marion, 404 U.S. 307, 324 (1971); United States v. Mayer, 503 F.3d 740, 747 (9th Cir. 2007); United States v. Benshop, 138 F.3d 1229, 1232 (8th Cir. 1998); United States v. West, 58 F.3d 133, 136 (5th Cir. 1995); United States v. Manning, 56 F.3d 1188, 1194 (9th Cir. 1995).

[226] United States v. Burke, 425 F.3d 400, 412-13 (7th Cir. 2005); United States v. Spillone, 879 F.2d 514, 524 (9th Cir. 1989); United States v. Levine, 700 F.2d 1176, 1180 (8th Cir. 1983); but not where there is no evidence that the government was aware the testimony was false, United States v. Strouse, 286 F.3d 767, 772 (5th Cir. 2002).

[227] United States v. Chen, 933 F.2d 793, 796-97 (11th Cir. 1991)("[a] perjury trap is created when the government calls a witness before the grand jury for the primary reason of obtaining testimony from him in order to prosecute him later for perjury"); United States v. Brown, 49 F.3d 1162, 1168 (6th Cir. 1995). As with most of the due process grounds, the perjury trap is most often spoken of in the abstract in a case where the court finds no due process violation.

[228] Goodrich v. Hall, 448 F.3d 45, 50 (1st Cir. 2006)(parallel citations omitted)("'An indictment returned by a legally constituted and unbiased grand jury . . . if valid on its face, is enough to call for trial of the charge on the merits.'" Costello v. United States, 350 U.S. 359, 363 (1956)").

[229] United States v. Williams, 504 U.S. 36, 46 (1992)("Rule 6 of the Federal Rules of Criminal Procedure contains a number of such rules, providing, for example, that 'no person other than the jurors may be present while the grand jury is deliberating or voting,' Rule 6(d), and placing strict controls on disclosure of 'matters occurring before the grand jury,' Rule 6(e). Additional standards of behavior for prosecutors (and others) are set forth in the United States Code. (See 18 U.S.C. §§6002, 6003 (setting forth procedures for granting a witness immunity from prosecution; §1623 (criminalizing false declarations before the grand jury); §2515 (prohibiting grand jury use of unlawfully intercepted wire or oral communications); §1622 (criminalization of perjury). . . ." 504 U.S. at 46 n.6).

[230] Bank of Nova Scotia v. United States, 487 U.S. 250, 256 (1988), quoting United States v. Mechanik, 475 U.S. at 78 (O'Connor, J., concurring); United States v. Vincent, 416 F.3d 593, 601 (7th Cir. 2005)("Even if errors in the grand jury proceedings would have justified the district court in dismissing the indictment prior to trial, the petit jury's subsequent conviction of Vincent rendered these

errors harmless beyond a reasonable doubt"); United States v. Sigma Industries, Inc., 244 F.3d 841, 874 (11th Cir. 2001); People v. Palomo, 35 F.3d 368, 371-72 (9th Cir. 1994).

[231] United States v. Williams, 504 U.S. 56, 64 (1992), citing, United States v. Mechanik, 475 U.S. 66, 71-2 (1986) and Bank of Nova Scotia v. United States, 487 U.S. 250, 256 (1988).

[232] Bank of Nova Scotia v. United States, 487 U.S. at 254; United States v. Lennick, 18 F.3d 814, 817-18 (9th Cir. 1994).

[233] United States v. Mechanik, 475 U.S. 66, 73 (1986); Goodrich v. Hall, 448 F.3d 45, 50 (1st Cir. 2006) ("The circumstances justifying dismissal of the indictment after conviction must be so severe, the prosecutorial misconduct so blatant, as to call into doubt the fundamental fairness of the judicial process"); United States v. Flores-Rivera, 56 F.3d 319 (1st Cir. 1995); United States v. Mills, 995 F.2d 480, 487 (4th Cir. 1993); cf., United States v. McDonald, 61 F.3d 248, 252-53 (4th Cir. 1995).

[234] United States v. Williams, 504 U.S. at 46-7 ("We did not hold in Bank of Nova Scotia, however, that the courts' supervisory power could be used, not merely as a means of enforcing or vindicating legally compelled standards of prosecutorial conduct before the grand jury, but as a means of prescribing those standards of professional conduct in the first instance. . . . Because the grand jury is an institution separate from the courts, over whose functioning the courts do not preside, we think it clear that, as a general matter at least, no such `supervisory' judicial authority exists. . . ") (emphasis of the Court).

[235] United States v. Williams, 504 U.S. at 45; United States v. Mahalick, 498 F.3d 475, 479 (7th Cir. 2007); Unuited States v. Casas, 425 F.3d 23, 37-8 (1st Cir. 2005); United States v. Waldon, 363 F.3d 1103, 1109 (11th Cir. 2004); United States v. Angel, 355 F.3d 462, 475 (6th Cir. 2004); United States v. Haynes, 216 F.3d 789, 798 (9th Cir. 2000);.

[236] United States v. Warren, 16 F.3d 247, 252-53 (8th Cir. 1994); United States v. Zangger, 848 F.2d 923, 925 (8th Cir. 1988); United States v. Buchanan, 787 F.2d 477, 487 (10th Cir. 1986).

[237] United States v. Hughson, 488 F.Supp.2d 835, 845 (D. Minn. 2007).

[238] United States v. Stein, 429 F.Supp.2d 633, 639-40 (S.D.N.Y. 2006), citing, Bank of Nova Scotia v. United States, 487 U.S. 250, 258-59 (1988).

[239] United States v. Singer, 660 F.2d 1295, 1302 (8th Cir. 1981); United States v. Levine, 457 F.2d 1186, 1189 (10th Cir. 1972); United States v. Conley, 826 F.Supp. 1533, 1534 (W.D.Pa. 1993).

[240] United States v. York, 428 F.3d 1325, 1331-332 (11th Cir. 2005).

[241] United States v. Vincent, 416 F.3d 593, 600 (7th Cir. 2005); United States v. Lamantia, 59 F.3d 705, 707-8 (7th Cir. 1995); United States v. Kilpatrick, 821 F.2d 1456, 1468-469 (10th Cir. 1987), aff'd on other grounds sub nom., Bank of Nova Scotia v. United States, 487 U.S. 250 (1987); United States v. Malatesta, 583 F.2d 748, 753-54 (5th Cir. 1978).

[242] United States v. Mechanik, 475 U.S. 66 (1986); United States v. Fowlie, 24 F.3d 1059, 1065-66 (9th Cir. 1994); United States v. Busch, 795 F.Supp. 866, 868 (N.D.Ill. 1992); United States v. Hart, 779 F.Supp. 883 (E.D.Mich. 1991).

[243] United States v. Costello, 350 U.S. 359, 363-64 (1956); United States v. Waldon, 363 F.3d 1103, 1109 (11th Cir. 2004); United States v. Roach, 28 F.3d 729, 739 (8th Cir. 1994); Wilkerson v. Whitley, 28 F.3d 498, 503 (5th Cir. 1994); Virgin Islands ex rel. A.M., 34 F.3d 153, 161 (3d Cir. 1994).

[244] United States v. Lombardozzi, 491 F.3d 61, 79 (2d Cir. 2007); United States v. Crockett, 435 F.3d 1305, 1316 (10th Cir. 2006); United States v. Burke, 425 F.3d 400, 412-13 (7th Cir. 2005); United States v. Soto-Beniquez, 356 F.3d 1, 24-5 (1st Cir. 2004); United States v. Haynes, 216 F.3d 789, 798 (9th Cir. 2000); United States v. McDonald, 61 F.3d 248, 252 (4th Cir. 1995); United States v. Claiborne, 765 F.2d 784, 791 (9th Cir. 1985); United States v. Adamo, 742 F.2d 917, 940 (6th Cir. 1984).

[245] United States v. Greve, 490 F.3d 566, 570-71 (7th Cir. 2007).

[246] United States v. Calandra, 414 U.S. 338, 349-52 (1974); United States v. Salazar, 323 F.3d 852, 856 (10th Cir. 2003); Wilkerson v. Whitley, 28 F.3d 498, 503 (5th Cir. 1994); Williams v. Poulous, 11 F.3d 271, 290 (1st Cir. 1993); Baylson v. Disciplinary Board, 975 F.2d 102, 110 n.3 (3d Cir. 1992).

[247] United States v. Haynes, 216 F.3d 789, 797-98 (9th Cir. 2000)("Haynes and Denton also argue that the district court should have exercised its supervisory power to dismiss the indictment on the ground that the government engaged in various acts of misconduct before the grand jury. To the extent that their argument is based on privileged testimony improperly elicited from Fairbanks [defense counsel's investigator], the challenge fails because a grand

jury is permitted to consider evidence obtained in violation of a privilege, whether the privilege is established by the Constitution, statute, or the common law. See United States v. Calandra, 414 U.S. 338, 346 (1974)“).

[248] United States v. Williams, 644 F.2d 950, 952 (2d Cir. 1981)(where the violations were not “wholesale”); United States v. Helstoski, 635 F.2d 200, 205-206 (3d Cir. 1980).

[249] United States v. Overmyer, 899 F.2d 457, 465 (6th Cir. 1990); United States v. Cronic, 675 F.2d 1126, 1130 (10th Cir. 1982); United States v. Leverage Funding Systems Inc., 637 F.2d 645, 649 (9th Cir. 1980).

[250] Rinaldi v. United States, 434 U.S. 22, 30 (1977); United States v. Romero, 360 F.3d 1248, 1251 (10th Cir. 2004); United States v. Gonzalez, 58 F.3d 459, 461 (9th Cir. 1995); United States v. Smith, 55 F.3d 157, 159 (4th Cir. 1995); United States v. Cockrell, 353 .Supp.2d 762, 768 (N.D.Tex. 2005).

[251] United States v. Soriano-Jarquin, 492 F.3d 495, 503 (4th Cir. 2007); United States v. Colombo, 852 F.2d 19, 24-6 (1st Cir. 1988); United States v. Dyal, 868 F.2d 424, 429 (11th Cir. 1989); United States v. Reardon, 787 F.2d 512, 518 (10th Cir. 1986).

[252] Vasquez v. Hillery, 474 U.S. 254, 263 (1986), citing Judge Friendly’s dissent in United States v. Ciambrone, 601 F.2d 616, 629 (2d Cir. 1979). There Judge Friendly repeats the words of Judge Wisdom: By refusing to indict, the grand jury has the unchallengeable power to defend the innocent from government oppression by unjust prosecution. And it has the equally unchallengeable power to shield the guilty, should the whims of the jurors or their conscious or subconscious response to community pressures induce twelve or more jurors to give sanctuary to the guilty. United States v. Cox, 342 F.2d 167, 189-90 (5th Cir. 1965). Consistent with the independence of the grand jury, it need not indict everywhere it finds probable cause, United States v. Ciambrone, 601 F.2d 616, 629 (2d Cir. 1979), cited in Vasquez v. Hillary, 474 U.S. 254, 263 (1986); United States v. Cotton, 261 F.3d 397, 407 (4th Cir. 2001); United States v. Navarro-Vargas, 408 F.3d 1184, 1206 (9th Cir. 2005).

[253] F.R.Crim.P 6(e)(3)(C); United States v. Williams, 504 U.S. 36, 49 (1992); United States v. Thompson, 251 U.S. 407, 413-14 (1920); In re United States, 441 F.3d 44, 63 (1st Cir. 2006); United States v. Claiborne, 765 F.2d 784, 793-94 (9th Cir. 1985); United States v. Pabian, 704 F.2d 1533, 1537 (11th Cir. 1983); In re Grand Jury

Proceedings, 658 F.2d 782, 783 (10th Cir. 1981); United States v. Gakoumis, 624 F.Supp. 655, 656 (E.D.Pa. 1985).

[254] United States v. Marcucci, 299 F.3d 1156, 1159 (9th Cir. 2002).

[255] See generally, Beale et al., GRAND JURY LAW AND PRACTICE, §§2.1 to 2.8 (1998 and 2007-2008 Supp.); Brenner and Shaw, FEDERAL GRAND JURY: A GUIDE TO LAW AND PRACTICE, §3.4 (2d ed. 2006); Stern, Revealing Misconduct by Public Officials Through Grand Jury Reports, 136 UNIVERSITY OF PENNSYLVANIA LAW REVIEW 73 (1987); Reviving Federal Grand Jury Presentments, 103 YALE LAW JOURNAL 1333 (1994); The Grand Jury Report as an Infringement on Private Rights, 23 HASTINGS LAW JOURNAL 561 (1972).

[256] 4 Blackstone, COMMENTARIES 275 (1813 ed.). Reports, on the other hand, involved statements of the grand jury on the conduct of the King's officials and the conditions of the public jails and highways. Over time, however, grand jury reports came to include those "presentments" upon which the grand jury had voted to indict but which could not be considered indictments because the attorney for the government would not sign them, In re Grand Jury January, 1969, 315 F.Supp. 662 (D.Md. 1970).

[257] Some state grand juries have more extensive reporting authority, see e.g., Adding Bite to the Watchdog's Bark: Reforming the California Civil Grand Jury System, 28 PACIFIC LAW JOURNAL 1115 (1997).

[258] In re Grand Jury Sitting in Cedar Rapids, Iowa, 734 F.Supp. 875, 876 (N.D. Iowa 1990); United States v. Christian, 660 F.2d 892 (3d Cir. 1981); Application of Jordan, 439 F.Supp. 199 (S.D.W.Va. 1977); United States v. Briggs, 514 F.2d 794 (5th Cir. 1975); In re Report and Recommendation of June 5, 1972 Grand Jury, 370 F.Supp. 1219 (D.D.C. 1974); Application of Johnson, 484 F.2d 791 (7th Cir. 1973); In re Presentment of Special Grand Jury Impaneled January, 1969, 315 F.Supp. 662 (D.Md. 1970); United States v. Cox, 342 F.2d 167, 188-89 (5th Cir. 1965)(Wisdom, J. concurring); In re Petition for Disclosure of Evidence Before the October 1959 Grand Jury, 184 F.Supp. 38 (E.D.Va. 1960); contra, Application of United Electrical, Radio and Machine Workers, 111 F.Supp. 858 (S.D.N.Y. 1953).

[259] In re Grand Jury Sitting in Cedar Rapids, Iowa, 734 F.Supp. 875, 876 (N.D. Iowa 1990), quoting In re Report of the Grand Jury Proceedings Filed on June 15, 1972, 479 F.2d 458, 460 n.2 (5th Cir.

1973); In re Grand Jury Proceedings (Rocky Flats), 813 F.Supp. 1451, 1466 (D.Colo. 1992).

[260] In re Petition for Disclosure of Evidence Before the October 1959 Grand Jury, 184 F.Supp. 38 (E.D.Va. 1960).

[261] F.R.Crim.P. 6(g)("A grand jury must serve until the court discharges it. . ."); Korman v. United States, 486 F.2d 926, 933 (7th Cir. 1973); Petition of A and H Transportation Inc., 319 F.2d 69, 71 (4th Cir. 1963); In re Investigation of World Arrangements, etc., 107 F.Supp. 628, 629 (D.D.C. 1952).

[262] What Do You Do With a Runaway Grand Jury? A Discussion of the Problems and Possibilities Opened Up by the Rocky Flats Grand Jury Investigation, 71 SOUTHERN CALIFORNIA LAW REVIEW 617 (1998); Roots, If It's Not a Runaway, It's Not a Real Grand Jury, 33 CREIGHTON LAW REVIEW 821 (2000).

In: The Federal Grand Jury
Editor: C. Doyle
ISBN: 978-1-60456-985-8

Chapter 2

HANDBOOK FOR FEDERAL GRAND JURORS

PURPOSE OF THIS HANDBOOK

This Handbook will acquaint persons who have been selected to serve on a federal grand jury with the general nature and importance of their role as grand jurors. It explains some of the terms that grand jurors will encounter during their service and offers some suggestions helpful to them in performing this important public service. It is intended that this Handbook will, to a degree, repeat and provide a permanent record of much of the information presented in the grand jury orientation film, The People's Panel, which in most districts is shown to grand jurors at the commencement of their service. Grand jurors are encouraged to refer to this Handbook periodically throughout their service to reacquaint themselves with their duties and responsibilities.

This Handbook is designed as an aid only to persons serving on a federal - not a state - grand jury. The federal grand jury is concerned only with federal crimes; it derives its authority from the Constitution of the United States, national laws, and the rules of the federal courts. There are also grand juries impaneled in many of the states, but those grand juries investigate only state crimes; they derive their authority from the constitutions, laws, and rules of court of the states where they are impaneled.

ORIGIN AND HISTORY OF THE GRAND JURY

The grand jury has a long and honorable tradition. It was recognized in the Magna Carta, the first English constitutional document, which King John granted in 1215 at the demand of his subjects. The first English grand jury consisted of twelve men selected from the knights or other freemen, who were summoned to inquire into crimes alleged to have been committed in their local community. Thus, grand jurors originally functioned as accusers or witnesses, rather than as judges.

Over the years, the hallmarks of our modern grand jury developed in England. For example, grand jury proceedings became secret, and the grand jury became independent of the Crown. As a result, a grand jury is able to vote an indictment or refuse to do so, as it deems proper, without regard to the recommendations of judge, prosecutor, or any other person. This independence from the will of the government was achieved only after a long hard fight. It can best be illustrated by the celebrated English case involving the Earl of Shaftasbury, who, in 1681, fell under the suspicion of the Crown. Displeased with him, the Crown presented to the grand jury a proposed bill of indictment for high treason and recommended that it be voted and returned. After hearing the witnesses, the grand jury voted against the bill of indictment and returned it to the King, holding that it was not true.

When the English colonists came to America, they brought with them many of the institutions of the English legal system, including the grand jury. Thus, the English tradition of the grand jury was well established in the American colonies long before the American Revolution. Indeed, the colonists used it as a platform from which to assert their independence from the pressures of colonial governors. In 1735, for example, the Colonial Governor of New York demanded that a grand jury indict for libel John Zenger, editor of a newspaper called "The Weekly Journal," because he had held up to scorn certain acts of the Royal Governor. The grand jury flatly refused.

The grand jury as an institution was so firmly established in the traditions of our forebears that they included it in the Bill of Rights. The Fifth Amendment to the Constitution of the United States provides in part that "(n)o person shall be held to answer for a capital, or otherwise infamous crime, unless on a presentment or indictment of a Grand Jury . . . ." Moreover, the grand jury system is also recognized in the constitutions of many of the states of the Union.

NATURE OF THE GRAND JURY

The powers and functions of the federal grand jury differ from those of the federal trial jury, which is called the petit jury. The petit jury listens to the evidence offered by the prosecution and the defense (if it chooses to offer any) during a criminal trial and returns a verdict of guilty or not guilty. The grand jury, on the other hand, does not determine guilt or innocence, but only whether there is probable cause to believe that a crime was committed and that a specific person or persons committed it. If the grand jury finds probable cause to exist against a person suspected of having committed the crime, then it will return a written statement of the charges called an "indictment." After that, the person will go to trial.

The grand jury normally hears only that evidence presented by a government attorney which tends to show the commission of a crime. The government attorney usually is the United States Attorney or and Assistant United States Attorney in the federal district. The grand jury must determine from this evidence, and usually without hearing evidence for the defense, whether the person being investigated by the government should be tried for a serious federal crime, referred to in the Bill of Rights as an "infamous crime." An infamous crime is one which may be punished by imprisonment for more than one year. As a general rule, no one can be prosecuted for a serious crime unless the grand jury decides that the evidence it has heard so requires. In this way, the grand jury operates both as a "sword," authorizing the government's prosecution of suspected criminals, and also as a "shield," protecting citizens from unwarranted or inappropriate prosecutions. The person being investigated by the government may, however, waive grand jury proceedings and agree to be prosecuted by a written charge of crime called an information.

The grand jury is not completely free to compel a trial of anyone it chooses. The government attorney must sign the indictment before one may be prosecuted. Thus, the government and the grand jury act as checks upon each other. This assures that neither may arbitrarily wield the awesome power to indict a person of a crime.

1. The Grand Jury's Tasks

As stated above, the federal grand jury's function is to determine whether the person being investigated by the government shall be tried for a serious federal crime alleged to have been committed within the district where it sits. Matters may be brought to its attention in three ways: (1) by the government attorney; (2) by the court that impaneled it; and (3) from the personal knowledge of a member of the grand jury or from matters properly brought to a member's personal attention. In all these cases, the grand jury must hear evidence before taking action.

After it has received evidence against the person being investigated, the grand jury must decide whether the evidence presented justifies an indictment, or "true bill," which is the formal criminal charge returned by the grand jury. Upon the indictment's being filed in court, that person must either plead guilty or nolo contendere or stand trial.

If the evidence does not persuade the grand jury that there is probable cause to believe the person being investigated committed a crime, the grand jury will vote a "no bill," or "not a true bill." When this occurs, that person is not required to plead to a criminal charge, and no trial is required.

2. Investigation

The major portion of the grand jury's work is concerned with evidence brought to its attention by the government attorney. The grand jury may consider additional matters otherwise brought to its attention, but should consult with the government attorney or the court before undertaking a formal investigation of such matters. This is necessary because the grand jury has no investigative staff, and legal assistance will be necessary in the event an indictment is voted.

It should be borne in mind that a federal grand jury can take action only upon federal crimes that have been committed within the district in which it has been impaneled. Furthermore, a federal grand jury (except a special grand jury impaneled under 18 U.S.C. §§ 3331-3334) is not authorized to investigate situations involving the conduct of individuals, public officials, agencies or institutions that the grand jury believes is subject to mere criticism rather than a violation of federal criminal statutes. Its concern must be devoted solely to ascertaining whether there is probable cause to believe that a federal crime has been committed and to report accordingly to the court.

SELECTION OF GRAND JURORS

Federal law requires that a grand jury be selected at random from a fair cross section of the community in the district or division in which the federal grand jury convenes. Thus, all citizens have an equal opportunity and obligation to serve.

Pursuant to law, the names of prospective grand jurors are drawn at random from lists of registered voters or lists of actual voters, or other sources when necessary, under procedures designed to ensure that all groups in the community will have a fair chance to serve. Those persons whose names have been drawn and who are not exempt or excused from service are summoned to appear for duty as grand jurors. When these persons appear before the court, the presiding judge may consider any further requests to be excused. The judge will then direct the selection of 23 qualified persons to become the members of the grand jury.

ORGANIZATION, OATH, AND OFFICERS OF THE FEDERAL GRAND JURY

After the proper number of persons have been qualified as grand jurors, the court will appoint one of them to be the foreperson, or presiding officer, of the grand jury. A deputy foreperson will also be appointed, so that he or she can act as presiding officer in the foreperson's absence.

The foreperson, the deputy foreperson, and the remaining members of the grand jury are sworn in by the Clerk of the Court. Those persons who do not wish to swear may affirm.

The oath taken by the grand jurors binds them to inquire diligently and objectively into all federal crimes committed within the district of which they have or may obtain evidence and to conduct such inquiry without malice, fear, ill will, or other emotion.

After the grand jurors have been sworn, the presiding judge advises the grand jury of its obligations and how best to perform its duties. This is called the charge to the grand jury. Careful attention must be paid to the charge, for it and any additional instructions that may be given by the court contain the rules and directions the grand jury must follow during its term of service.

After the grand jury has been charged, it is taken to the grand jury room, where it will hear testimony and consider documentary evidence in the cases brought to its attention by the government attorney.

PROCEDURE

1. Quorum

Sixteen of the 23 members of the grand jury constitute a quorum for the transaction of business. If fewer than this number are present, even for a moment, the proceedings of the grand jury must stop. This shows how important it is that each grand juror conscientiously attend the meetings. If an emergency will prevent a grand juror's attendance at the meeting, he or she must promptly advise the grand jury foreperson. If the juror's absence will prevent the grand jury from acting, the grand juror should, if at all possible, attend the meeting.

2. Evidence Before the Grand Jury

Much of the grand jury's time is spent hearing testimony by witnesses and examining documentary or other evidence in order to determine whether such evidence justifies an indictment.

Each federal court district has a United States Attorney whose duty it is to represent the United States in federal matters within the district and to prosecute those accused of federal crimes. In the usual case, the United States Attorney or one of the Assistant United States Attorneys will present the evidence of alleged violations of the law to the grand jury. These government attorneys also advise grand jurors as to what witnesses should be called and what documentary evidence should be produced for examination by the grand jury. The grand jury may ask that additional witnesses be called if it believes this necessary. The government attorney will also prepare the formal written indictments that the grand jury wishes to present. But a government attorney may not remain in the room while the grand jury deliberates and votes on an indictment.

3. Questioning the Witness

Witnesses are called to testify one after another. Upon appearing to give testimony, each witness will be sworn by the grand jury foreperson or, in the foreperson's absence, the deputy foreperson. The witness will then be questioned. Ordinarily, the government attorney questions the witness first, followed next by the foreperson of the grand jury. Then, the other members of the grand jury may question the witness.

All questions asked of each witness must be relevant and proper, relating only to the case under investigation. If doubt should arise as to whether a question is appropriate, the advice of the government attorney may be sought. If necessary, a ruling may be obtained from the court.

Because of the need for secrecy, described in more detail in the following section, the law forbids anyone other than authorized persons from being present in the grand jury room while evidence is being presented. This means that only the grand jury, the government attorney, the witness under examination, the court reporter, and an interpreter, if required, may be present. If an indictment should ultimately be voted, the presence of unauthorized persons in the grand jury room could invalidate it.

Occasionally, prior to answering a question, a witness may ask to leave the grand jury room to consult with his or her attorney. The grand jury can not hold such conduct against a witness, for every witness has the right to confer with counsel even though counsel may not be present in the grand jury room. In fact, a witness may confer with counsel after each question, as long as he or she does not make a mockery of the proceedings or does not, by such, make an attempt to impede the orderly progress of the grand jury investigation.

Additionally, a witness who is appearing before the grand jury may invoke the Fifth Amendment privilege against self-incrimination and refuse to answer a question. In such a situation, the grand jurors may bring the matter before the court in order to obtain a ruling as to whether or not the answer may be compelled and under what circumstances.

4. Calling the Person Being Investigated by the Government as a Witness

Normally, neither the person being investigated by the government nor any witness on behalf of that person will testify before the grand jury.

Upon request, preferably in writing, the person being investigated by the government may be given the opportunity by the grand jury to appear before it. Such person who does so appear cannot be forced to testify because of the constitutional privilege against self-incrimination. If the grand jury attempts to force the person being investigated to testify, an indictment returned against that person may be nullified.

Because the appearance of the person being investigated by the government before the grand jury may raise complicated legal problems, a grand jury that desires to request or to permit that person to appear before it should consult with the government attorney and, if necessary, the court before proceeding.

Even if the person being investigated by the government is willing to testify voluntarily, that the person must be advised of the right not to testify. Also, he or she is required to sign a formal waiver of this right. The grand jury should be completely satisfied that the person being investigated fully understands what he or she is doing.

5. The Evidence Needed Before a "'True Bill" May Be Voted

It is the responsibility of the grand jury to weigh the evidence presented to it in order to determine whether this evidence, usually without any explanation being offered by the person being investigated by the government, persuades it that there is probable cause to believe that a crime has been committed and that the person being investigated was the person who committed it. Remember that the grand jury is not responsible for determining whether the person being investigated is guilty beyond a reasonable doubt, but only whether there is sufficient evidence of probable cause to justify bringing the that person to trial. Only the evidence presented to the grand jury in the grand jury room may be considered in determining whether to vote an indictment.

6. Deliberations

When the grand jury has received all the evidence on a given charge, all persons other than the members of the grand jury or an interpreter necessary to assist a juror who is hearing or speech impaired, must leave the room so that the grand jury may begin its deliberations. The presence of any other person in the grand jury room while the grand jury deliberates or votes may nullify an indictment returned on the accusation.

After all persons other than the grand jury members and any interpreter for a hearing or speech impaired juror have left the room, the foreperson will ask the grand jury members to discuss and vote upon the question of whether the evidence persuades the grand jury that a crime has probably been committed by the person person being investigated by the government and that an indictment should be returned. Every grand juror has the right to express his or her view of the matter under consideration, and grand jurors should listen to the comments of all their fellow grand jurors before making up their mind. Only after each grand juror has been given the opportunity to be heard will the vote be taken. It should be remembered that at least 16 jurors must be present and 12 members must vote in favor of the indictment before it may be returned.

The foreperson of the grand jury must keep a record of the number of jurors concurring in the finding of every indictment and file the record with the Clerk of the Court. If an indictment is found, the grand jury, or its foreperson or deputy foreperson, will report it to the judge or a magistrate judge in open court. It will likewise report any "not true bills," or decisions not to indict. A decision not to indict should immediately be reported to the court in writing by the foreperson so that the person being investigated by the government may promptly be released from jail or freed from bail.

SECRECY

The law imposes upon each grand juror a strict obligation of secrecy. This obligation is emphasized in the oath each grand juror takes and in the charge given to the grand jury by the judge.

The tradition of secrecy continues as a vital part of the grand jury system for many reasons. It protects the grand jurors from being subjected to pressure by persons who may be subjects of investigations by the grand jury or associates of such persons. It prevents the escape of those against whom an indictment is being considered. It encourages witnesses before the grand jury to give full and truthful information as to the commission of a crime. It also prevents tampering with or intimidation of such witnesses before they testify at trial. Finally, it prevents the disclosure of investigations that result in no action by the grand jury and avoids any stigma the public might attach to one who is the subject of a mere investigation by the grand jury.

Essentially, the grand jury may disclose matters occurring before it only to the government attorneys for use in the performance of their duties, but even the government attorneys may not be informed of what took place during the grand jury's deliberations and voting. The only other time matters occurring before the grand jury may be disclosed to anyone is when disclosure is ordered by the court in the interests of justice. Disclosure of such matters may never be made to grand juror's friends or family, including a grand juror's spouse.

Protection of Grand Jurors

The secrecy imposed upon grand jurors is a major source of protection for them. In addition, no inquiry may be made to learn what grand jurors said or how they voted, except upon order of the court.

The law gives the members of a grand jury broad immunity for actions taken by them within the scope of their authority as grand jurors.

Because of this immunity, all grand jurors must perform their duties with the highest sense of responsibility.

Practical Suggestions for Grand Jurors

Each grand juror should attend the grand jury sessions regularly, in order to ensure that a quorum of 16 members will be present to conduct the grand jury's business.

Each grand juror should be on time for each meeting so that others are not kept waiting.

The time of meetings should be scheduled so as to be convenient for the grand jury, the government attorney, and the witnesses.

Witnesses should be treated courteously when they appear before the grand jury. Questions should be put to them in an orderly fashion. The government attorney should complete his or her questioning of each witness before the foreperson asks questions. The remaining grand jurors will then have a chance to ask relevant and proper questions.

Each grand juror has an equal voice in determining whether or not an indictment should be returned. Therefore, it is important that all grand jurors pay close attention to the testimony and other evidence presented.

Each grand juror must be absolutely fair in his or her judgment of the facts. Otherwise, the grand juror will defeat the democratic purpose the grand jury is designed to serve.

During deliberations on a case, each grand juror should feel free to express his or her opinion based upon the evidence.

Each juror has equal duties and responsibilities, and each is entitled to be satisfied with the evidence before being called upon to vote. No juror has the right to dismiss a witness or to shut off proper discussion if other jurors wish to pursue the matter further.

No grand jury should undertake to investigate matters outside its proper scope merely because someone suggested an investigation, or because the investigation would be interesting.

No grand juror should discuss the cases under investigation with anyone, except fellow grand jurors and the government attorney, and then only in the grand jury room. Of course, the grand jurors may always seek the advice of the judge.

Finally, every citizen who is selected to serve on a federal grand jury should bring to this task the determination to participate in a responsible manner and to make every effort to ensure that the grand jury will be a credit not only to the community it represents but to the United States.

Glossary of Terms

Charge to the Grand Jury

Given by the judge presiding over the selection and organization of the grand jury, the charge is the court's instructions to the grand jury as to its duties, functions, and obligations, and how to best perform them.

Deliberations

The discussion by the grand jury members as to whether or not to return an indictment on a given charge against an person being investigated by the government. During deliberations no one except the grand jury members or an interpreter for a hearing or speech impaired juror may be present.

District

The geographical area over which the federal district court where the grand jury sits and the grand jury itself have jurisdiction. The territorial limitations of the district will be explained to the grand jury by the district judge.

Evidence

Testimony of witnesses, documents, and exhibits as presented to the grand jury by a government attorney or otherwise properly brought before it. In some instances, the person person being investigated by the government may also testify.

Federal

The national government as distinguished from the state governments.

Government Attorney

Usually the United States Attorney or an Assistant United States Attorney in the federal district.

Grand Jurors' Immunity

Immunity is granted to all grand jurors for their authorized actions while serving on a federal grand jury and means that no grand juror may be penalized for actions taken within the scope of his or her service as a grand juror.

Indictment

The written formal charge of a crime by the grand jury, returned when 12 or more grand jurors vote in favor of it.

Information

The written formal charge of crime by the government attorney, filed against the person being investigated who, if charged with a serious crime, must have knowingly waived the requirements that the evidence first be presented to a grand jury.

"No Bill"

Also referred to as "not a true bill," the "no bill" is the decision by the grand jury not to indict a person being investigated by the government.

Petit Jury

The trial jury, composed of 12 members, that hears a case after indictment and renders a verdict or decision after hearing the prosecution's entire case and whatever evidence the defendant chooses to offer.

Person Being Investigated by the Government

The person suspected of having committed a federal crime. Use of this term does not imply the person being investigated is guilty of any crime. After a person is indicted by the grand jury, that person is referred to as the "defendant."

Probable Cause

The finding necessary in order to return an indictment against the person being investigated by the government of a federal crime. A finding of probable cause is proper only when the evidence presented to the grand jury, without any explanation being offered by the person being investigated, persuades 12 or more grand jurors that a federal crime has probably been committed by that person.

Quorum for Grand Jury to Conduct Business

Sixteen of the 23 members of a federal grand jury must at all times be present at a grand jury session in order for the grand jury to be able to conduct business.

United States Attorney

The chief legal officer for the United States government in each federal district.

INDEX

D

E

F

G

P

Q

R

S

T

U

V

W

Y